Teachers' Professional Duties
and
Teachers' Legal Liabilities and Responsibilities

Designed specifically for both Newly Qualified Teachers and students completing courses of Initial Teacher Training, that contains information, advice and
commentary relating to Standard 1.8 (Statutory Frameworks) of *Professional
Values and Practice* of *Qualifying to Teach: Professional Standards for Qualified
Teacher Status* and *Requirements for Initial Teacher Training* (DfES/TTA, 2002).

Teachers' Professional Duties
and
Teachers' Legal Liabilities and Responsibilities

Compiled by Nigel Gates
Education Department
University of Hertfordshire

EDUCATION DEPARTMENT
UNIVERSITY OF HERTFORDSHIRE

First published in Great Britain in 2003 by
Education Department
University of Hertfordshire
College Lane, Hatfield, Hertfordshire
AL10 9AB

British Library Cataloguing-in-Publication-Data.
A catalogue record for this book is available from the British Library.

ISBN 1 898534 29 2

Designed by Geoff Green@Geoff Green Book Design, Cambridge CB4 5RA.
Printed in Great Britain by St Edmundsbury Press, Bury St Edmunds IP33 3TZ

Contents

Protecting Children

Other Relevant Documents

Other information, guidance and legislation which teachers should be aware of

Foreword

It is crucial that teachers are well supported in order for them to achieve the highest possible standards in their profession. A handbook such as this one provides an accessible and informative guide to the professional values and practice which teachers are committed to upholding. It also provides a comprehensive digest of the formal context of their work in schools and other settings. Useful as a reference document to dip into, it will provide trainees, newly qualified teachers and others with ready access to the statutory legal frameworks for the profession.

I am pleased to note the inclusion of the General Teaching Council's Code of Professional Values and Practice for Teachers. The Council is keen to work in partnership to uphold and promote high standards of professionalism and we welcome this acknowledgement. Teachers need to have ownership of these standards to enable the profession to achieve self-regulation, in the public interest.

Carol Adams.

CAROL ADAMS
Chief Executive
General Teaching Council for England

Author's Note to 3rd Edition

The first edition of this booklet was originally produced in 1998 for students who were completing their courses of Initial Teacher Training in the Education Department of the University of Hertfordshire. Under 'Other professional requirements' of Section D of Annex A of the Department for Education and Employment (DfEE) Circular 4/98, all newly qualified teachers were required to have a working knowledge of the legal aspects of teachers' professional duties, liabilities and responsibilities. The main purpose of the 1998 booklet was to bring together, in a single, easy-to-read document, all relevant material on aspects of the law as required by the DfEE and published in its Circular 4/98. So that some new legislation and other important legal changes (in particular, the establishment of the General Teaching Council for England) could be included, a second edition was produced in 1999.

However, the DfEE Circular 4/98 is no longer the relevant guidance document. The Requirements for Initial Teacher Training have been thoroughly revised by the Department for Education and Skills (DfES) and the Teacher Training Agency (TTA). New *"Guidance on the Requirements for Initial Teacher Training"* was published, by the TTA, in April 2002 and the new Standards for the Award of Qualified Teacher Status (QTS) took effect from September 2002. Therefore it was necessary to revise the booklet completely to take into account the new Standard. This is Standard 1.8 of Professional Values and Practice: *"the statutory frameworks that all teachers must be aware of and work within"*.

The Teacher Training Agency's *"Handbook on the Guidance on the Standards for the Award of Qualified Teacher Status"* was published on the TTA website (www.canteach.gov.uk) at the end of June 2002. Although a "hard copy" of the Handbook, containing some minor revisions, was scheduled to be published by the TTA at the end of October 2002, it should be noted that all references in this booklet to the *"Handbook on the Guidance on the Standards for the Award of Qualified Teacher Status"* relate to the June 2002 Internet version.

Some of the content of the third edition remains the same (as does the booklet's title), although it is recognised that the title no longer reflects the title of the new Standard. However, the structure of the third edition has been reorganised in sections reflecting the major divisions (Protecting Children, Special Educational Needs/Disability, Inclusion/Discrimination, Employment, and Other Relevant Documents) that are shown in the list of documents relating to the care and education of children and young people which accompanies Standard 1.8 in the *"Handbook on Guidance on the Standards for the award of QTS".* However, unlike the organisation of the TTA's list, the ordering in this booklet commences with employment because this seemed to be rather more logical. (After all, one must be employed as a teacher before any of the other sections really apply.)

Some of the matters discussed relate to more than one section. For example, aspects of health and safety are paralleled in connection with care and welfare. Furthermore, the chapters on discriminating according to sex, race or disability follow similar formats (because the legislation is so similar). Readers will also find some chapter titles duplicated. For example, the Sex Discrimination Act 1975 appears in the Employment and the Inclusion/Discrimination sections of this booklet. (In the Employment section aspects of sex discrimination in employment are described; in the Inclusion/Discrimination section the emphasis is on sex discrimination and pupils.) To avoid excessive cross-referencing, but at the expense of some repetition, information is duplicated in some sections.

Furthermore, where it is believed that it will be helpful to the reader, some additional information (such as information about the Criminal Records Bureau) has been included at the relevant point in the text although this is not on the TTA's list of suggested documents. It must be noted that the TTA's list is not exhaustive and, furthermore, several of the references have been discontinued and are no longer available. Some additional material (such as guidance on the writing of references) has been placed in the booklet's final section: 'Other information, guidance and legislation which teachers should be aware of'. The booklet's Bibliography also contains more references than those given by the TTA. The author has provided this additional material because it is felt that the subjects are ones that those completing courses of initial teacher training and Newly Qualified Teachers should all be aware of.

Those who compare this edition with the two earlier editions will at once notice that this edition is substantially longer, well over twice the size. This is because the 2002 DfES/TTA list of references is substantially longer than the DfEE 4/98 list of references. In order to provide a description and explanation of each of the many 2002 DfES/TTA references, this booklet contains much more detail than the earlier editions. An index has been added and everything possible has been done to make this edition as helpful and user-friendly as possible.

Finally, the government department responsible for education in England and Wales is named the Department for Education and Skills (DfES). However, over the last decade the Department has had two other, slightly different, names: the Department for Education (DfE) and, the Department for Education and Employment (DfEE). The Department produces a variety of publications and the document's reference number/title reflects the name of the Department at the time of publication. Although the Department is now the Department for Education and Skills (DfES), throughout this booklet, for the sake of clarity and accuracy, all references to Department publications (and the Department) are to the name that the Department had at the time of the document's publication.

I am extremely grateful to Professor Chris Cook for his assistance in the production of this handbook.

Nigel Gates

Introduction

Although this book is about the statutory legal frameworks which teachers must be aware of and work within, it is important to keep things in proportion. Teachers should never lose sight of their special function which is to introduce their pupils to information, ideas and skills, and to ensure that these are learnt. However, from the beginning of their career (and this also includes student teachers), teachers should always remember that, as a member of the teaching profession, they are expected always to act appropriately and to maintain the very highest professional standards.

Nearly all teachers behave professionally and sympathetically towards their pupils and have no cause to worry about the detail of the law. Unfortunately, and occasionally, circumstances arise that require special care. It is as well to be alert to this possibility and know what the law requires. Knowledge empowers rather than restricts and this booklet is intended to assist in this. It is certainly not the author's intention to undermine confidence in working with pupils and colleagues and the author hopes that the knowledge gained from this booklet will be positive and expansive rather than restricting. Those who act from a sense of professional responsibility are likely to benefit from the law rather than be restricted or, even worse, be condemned by it. Perhaps the most important implication of this document is that professionalism requires forethought, preparation and a degree of detachment that does not imply unconcern. Negligence and carelessness are not acceptable and it is worth remembering that, as a whole, society has become very much more litigious.

Because of the rather dense and complex nature of some of the legal material, this booklet should not be treated as a text that is to be absorbed at a single reading. Rather, it is probably best used as a document for reference alongside other course materials and teaching sessions during initial training. The author hopes that it will be particularly useful in schools, although it must be recognised that the law is not static and teachers should always be aware that new legislation may affect them and/or the children that they are responsible for. (The teacher unions are usually very good at making any such information known to their members.)

Although Parliament determines what an Act includes, the interpretation of the Acts is, in the end, the responsibility of the courts and, in this connection, your attention is drawn to the superiority of the courts. Furthermore, you will notice that the sharpness of the legislation varies: 190 teaching days per school year means exactly that - and neither 189 nor 191. On the other hand, the concept of "behaving reasonably" is more open to interpretation. The notion of what is **reasonable** is often used in law (such as "the reasonable direction of the head teacher" in the School Teachers' Pay and Conditions Document, a "reasonable working environment" in connection with an employee's place of employment, and the notion of "reasonable forseeability" in negligence cases). The acid test of what is reasonable, or what is reasonable behaviour, can often form the basis of a court or Employment Tribunal decision.

Teachers have wide-ranging responsibilities for the general welfare of both their pupils and their colleagues. However, as employees, teachers also have rights and responsibilities and it is important to note the very specific legal feature of the employer/employee relationship known as **vicarious liability**. This makes an employer liable for certain wrongs (such as negligence) of an employee while he/she is acting in the course of his/her employment – and this applies even if the employee was acting negligently or was disobeying the employer's instructions or procedures. Although vicarious liability is normally for civil wrongs, some criminal wrongs (such as Health and Safety and/or negligence) are also covered. Although a plaintiff may sue the employer, or the employee, or employer and employee jointly, it is the employer who will have to pay if the court or tribunal finds for the plaintiff and awards damages. Although, in almost all cases, the employer (the school or local education authority), rather than the individual, has to defend the action, the possibility nevertheless exists that individuals could find themselves defending their actions in the courts or at employment tribunals. For example, in several recent school pupil fatalities which occurred on "educational visits" (fatalities involving water activities), both the teacher as well as the school/local education authority have found themselves in court and, in at least two cases, both have been found guilty. (Furthermore, in the Inclusion/Discrimination section of this booklet discussing the Sex Discrimination Act 1975, also see the 1980s case of *Debell, Sevket and Teh – v – the London Borough of Bromley.*)

It should be pointed out that although it is unlawful to discriminate under United Kingdom law on the grounds of sex, race and disability, there is currently no such UK legislation covering discrimination on the grounds of age. However, the United Kingdom government has pledged to introduce legislation to combat age discrimination by 2006 and issued a Code of Good Practice in 1999.

Finally, in Acts of Parliament and in many legal documents, the convention is to use "he", "him" or "his"; in almost all cases, this must also be taken to mean "she" or "her". The author of this booklet understands the sensitivities involved but, because there are many sections which have been transcribed from legal documents, it would be difficult - and would have made the text extremely clumsy – to have replaced "he" with "he/she" and "him" with "him/her", etc, in every case. Please, therefore, do forgive the use of "he" etc. where it occurs. Furthermore, in the text of this document, all the sections written in italic script are text that has been copied verbatim from the relevant Act, Circular, etc

Professional Values and Practice, Standard 1.8 (the Statutory Frameworks teachers must be aware of and work within), from the Handbook to the Guidance on Standards for the Award of Qualified Teacher Status, DfEE/TTA, 2002

The text that follows is the full text and the accompanying list of documents of DfES/TTA Standard 1.8 of the new 2002 QTS Standards and has been placed here for reference purposes.

Those awarded Qualified Teacher Status must understand and uphold the professional code of the General Teaching Council for England by demonstrating that:

They are aware of, and work, within the statutory frameworks relating to teachers' responsibilities.

Scope

Teachers have an important role in the legal framework designed to protect both children and adults. Teachers are not expected to have a detailed knowledge of the whole legal framework, but they need to be aware of their own statutory responsibilities and where to gain information, support and assistance when they need it. They also need to be aware that they have rights and responsibilities as employees as well as teachers.

Trainee teachers will find it helpful to be aware of relevant aspects of the law, including the legal framework relating to professional conduct and conditions of service, to protect them from being perceived as acting unprofessionally or illegally. By knowing the extent of their responsibilities they will be helped to anticipate problems and avoid errors. In particular, trainee teachers need to develop an ability to judge when they may need advice, for example, on matters of child protection or confidentiality, and know how to seek it. This will be particularly important in areas such as the teacher's responsibilities under the SEN Code of Practice, or any contribution they may make to formal assessments.

Key documents

The Standard does not require trainee teachers to have read or internalised a full list of the statutory documents relating to the care and education of children and young people. There are many such documents. See end of this section for a selection of documents that have been provided for reference purposes only.

Evidence relevant to meeting the Standard

When judging trainees' practice, assessors will want to draw on observations of trainee teachers' teaching and the reports of school-based tutors for evidence about the professional judgements which trainee teachers make, and the advice they seek, in the course of their practical work with children, colleagues and parents. For example, does the trainee seek advice at an appropriate stage in relation to particular pupils' special educational needs? Does the trainee take appropriate responsibility for their own and pupils' safety during out-of-school visits or activities? There may be relevant evidence related to Standard 2.6 on seeking specialist SEN advice, Standard 3.3.8 on safe use of resources and Standard 3.3.9 on pupil discipline and behaviour management.

Trainee teachers' opportunities to demonstrate awareness of the statutory framework in their teaching will vary according to their particular experiences and the schools in which they are placed. Assessors will therefore wish to use a variety of means to establish trainees' level of understanding of how the statutory frameworks impact on their work. This could include discussions with the trainee and written assignments.

Documents relating to the care and education of children and young people

The following list of documents is provided for reference purposes only, and is likely to be useful to trainees in developing an awareness of the framework relating to teachers' responsibilities, and when thinking about the legal implications of any issues that might arise during their training and their teaching career.

Standard 1.8 does not require trainee teachers to have read or internalised a full list of documents relating to the care and education of children and young people.

Protecting Children

-   DfEE Circular 10/95: Protecting children from abuse: the role of the education service
-   DfEE Circular 11/95 Misconduct of Teachers and Workers with Children and Young Persons (NB document discontinued)
-   HMSO (1989) The Children Act: especially Section 3(5) on what is reasonable in safeguarding and promoting children's welfare
-   HMSO (2000) The Sexual Offences (Amendment) Act: Section 3
-   Home Office/DfEE/ DoH (1999) Working Together to Safeguard Children – A guide to inter-agency working to safeguard and promote the welfare of children
-   Home Office (1999) Caring for young people and the vulnerable? Guidance for preventing abuse of trust

Special Educational Needs/Disability

-   DfE Circular 9/94 – DHLAC (94)9: The Education of Children with Emotional and Behavioural Difficulties
-   DfEE/DoH Circular 14/96: Supporting Pupils with Medical Needs in School
-   DfEE (2001) SEN Code of Practice
-   HMSO (2001) The Special Educational Needs and Disability Act

Inclusion/discrimination

-   DfEE Circular 10/99, Social Inclusion: Pupil Support
-   DfEE (2001) Education of Young People in Public Care
-   DfEE Circular 3/97: What the Disability Discrimination Act

(DDA) 1995 means for Schools and LEAs (NB document discontinued)
- HMSO (1975) The Sex Discrimination Act
- HMSO (1976) The Race Relations Act
- HMSO (2000) The Race Relations (Amendment) Act
- HMSO (1995) The Disability Discrimination Act
- NGfL Inclusion website: www.inclusion.ngfl.gov.uk
- OFSTED (1999) Raising the Attainment of Minority Ethnic Pupils – School and LEA Responses
- OFSTED (2000) Evaluating Educational Inclusion – Guidance for Inspectors and Schools
- TTA (2000) Raising the Attainment of Minority Ethnic Pupils

Employment

- DfEE Circular 4/99: Physical and mental fitness to teach of teachers and of entrants to Initial Teacher Training
- HMSO (1974) The Health and Safety at Work Act: sections 7 and 8
- HMSO (1991) The School Teachers' Pay and Conditions Act
- DfEE Guidance Note 10/9/98 Recruitment and Selection Procedures: Vetting Teachers and Other Staff who will have Contact with Children (NB document discontinued)
- HMSO (1995) The Disability Discrimination Act
- CRE Code of Practice for the elimination of racial discrimination in employment: CRE website: www.cre.gov.uk

Other relevant documents

- DfEE Circular 10/98: Section 550A of The Education Act 1996: The Use of Force to Control or Restrain Pupils
- GTC(E) (2002) The Code of Professional Values and Practice for Teachers
- HMSO (1996) The Education Act: sections 548, 550A, 572
- HMSO (1997) The Education Act: section 4
- HMSO (1998) The Human Rights Act
- HMSO (1997) The Protection from Harassment Act
- HMSO (1998) The Public Interest Disclosure Act
- HMSO (1988) The Copyright, Designs and Patents Act
- Mental Health in Education. Promoting Children's Mental Health within Early Years and School Settings
  www.DfEs.gov.uk

Employment

1. Introductory Comments

As far as employment is concerned, it must be stated that the list of reference documents in the "Employment" section of the Guidance on the 2002 Standards for the Award of Qualified Teacher Status has several important omissions, in particular the Sex Discrimination Act 1975, the Race Relations Act 1976, and the Race Relations (Amendment) Act 2000. (These three Acts are, however, listed in the "Inclusion/Discrimination" section).

Although a teacher must be very careful not to discriminate against an individual pupil or particular groups of pupils (or other employee/s), teachers have specific rights, under discrimination legislation, both when seeking employment and as employees. Like all employees in the country (under the Sex Discrimination Act 1975, the Race Relations Act 1976, the Race Relations (Amendment) Act 2000, and the Disability Discrimination Act 1995), a teacher must not be discriminated against on grounds of sex, marital status, race or disability.

Therefore, in the Employment Section of this booklet, attention will be given to the Sex Discrimination Act 1975, the Race Relations Act 1976, and the Race Relations (Amendment) Act 2000, even though the "Employment" section of the Guidance on the 2002 Standards for the Award of Qualified Teacher Status does not list either of these two Acts.

Furthermore, although the Sexual Offences (Amendment) Act 2002 is listed in the "Protecting Children" section of the Guidance on the 2002 Standards for the Award of Qualified Teacher Status, it is not listed in the "Employment" section. However, because its provisions certainly affect teachers as employees, it will also receive attention in the Employment Section of this booklet. It is hoped that, at the risk of some duplication, the reader will find this to be helpful.

2. The Teacher's Professional Duties as set out in the current School Teachers' Pay and Conditions Document, issued under the School Teachers' Pay and Conditions Act 1991 including PART XII - Conditions of Employment of Teachers other than Head Teachers, and Part XI - Conditions of Employment of Advanced Skills Teachers and Fast Track Teachers

The School Teachers' Pay and Conditions Document, issued under the School Teachers' Pay and Conditions Act 1991, is a very important document indeed. Its provisions are given legal force by a Pay and Conditions Order and set the statutory conditions of employment of school teachers in all maintained schools, including grant-maintained schools, in England and Wales. The Pay and Conditions Document is revised annually and a copy is sent to every maintained school. A school's governing body must ensure that teachers have access to the latest Pay and Conditions Document (and to the associated DfES Pay and Conditions of Employment Circular).

In the DfEE 4/98 criteria it was deemed necessary to have *a working knowledge and understanding of the teacher's professional duties as set out in the current School Teachers' Pay and Conditions Document.* Surprisingly, this has been omitted from the DfES/TTA 2002 Standards for the Award of Qualified Teacher Status criteria. However, because all teachers have a statutory duty to carry out their professional duties, within the reasonable direction of their head teacher, this particular section has been retained in this booklet.

Broadly, to enable a teacher to discharge his/her professional duties (such as preparing lessons, marking pupils' work, and writing reports), the professional duties defined in the Pay and Conditions Document are that teachers (other than head teachers) may be required to:

- carry out reasonable instructions of the head teacher;

- teach – including planning and preparing, setting and marking of work,
- assessing, recording and reporting, etc;
- take part in other activities e.g. providing guidance and advice to pupils,
- meeting and consulting with parents, etc;
- prepare assessments and reports etc;
- participate in appraisal and undertake training and development;
- advise and co-operate with the head teacher and other teachers on the
- preparation and development of courses of study, methods of teaching
- and assessment, etc;
- maintain good order and discipline among the pupils and safeguard their health and safety;
- participate in staff meetings;
- cover for absent colleagues;
- participate in preparing pupils for public examinations and in the assessment of pupils in these examinations;
- participate in administrative and organisational tasks related to the duties described in this paragraph;
- attend school assemblies, register the attendance of pupils, and supervise pupils;
- work for 195 days in any school year, 190 days with pupils and 5 days when pupils are not present;
- work in the school up to a maximum of 1265 hours in every school year;
- work any additional hours as may be needed (outside school if necessary)

As well as sections on pay, the main section which teachers must be aware of and comply with is now *Part XII – Conditions of Employment of Teachers other than Head Teachers*. This describes in detail the **legally binding conditions of employment of teachers in all maintained schools**, and Part XII of the School Teachers' Pay and Conditions Document 2002 is reproduced, in full, below. (However, it is important to note that teachers who are either Advanced Skills Teachers or Fast Track Teachers do have certain additional conditions of employment and these are described in Part XI of the 2002 Document).

Part XII - Conditions of Employment of Teachers other than Head Teachers

Exercise of general professional duties

64.1   Subject to paragraph 42.6, 43.2, 43.3 and 66.2, a teacher who is not a head teacher shall carry out the professional duties of a teacher as circumstances may require:

64.1.1 if he is employed as a teacher in a school, under the reasonable direction of the head teacher of that school;

64.1.2 if he is employed by an authority on terms under which he is not assigned to any one school, under the reasonable direction of that authority and of the head teacher of any school in which he may for the time being be required to work as a teacher.

64.2   A teacher who has failed satisfactorily to complete an induction period and who is employed pursuant to regulation 16(5) of the Induction Regulations must only carry out such limited teaching duties as the Secretary of State determines pursuant to that regulation.

Exercise of particular duties

65.1   Subject to paragraph 42.6, 43.2, 43.3, and 64.2 a teacher employed as a teacher (other than a head teacher) in a school shall perform, in accordance with any directions which may reasonably be given to him by the head teacher from time to time, such particular duties as may reasonably be assigned to him.

65.2   A teacher employed by an authority on terms such as those described in paragraph 64.1.2 shall perform, in accordance with any direction which may reasonably be given to him from time to time by the authority or by the head teacher of any school in which he may for the time being be required to work as a teacher, such particular duties as may reasonably be assigned to him.

Professional duties

66.   Subject to paragraph 42.6, 43.2, 43.3, and 64.2 the following duties shall be deemed to be included in the professional

duties which a teacher (other than a head teacher) may be required to perform:

66.1 **Teaching:**

In each case having regard to the curriculum for the school:

66.1.1 planning and preparing courses and lessons;

66.1.2 teaching, according to their educational needs, the pupils assigned to him, including the setting and marking of work to be carried out by the pupil in school and elsewhere;

66.1.3 assessing, recording and reporting on the development, progress and attainment of pupils;

66.2 **Other activities:**

66.2.1 promoting the general progress and well-being of individual pupils and of any class or group of pupils assigned to him;

66.2.2 providing guidance and advice to pupils on educational and social matters and on their further education and future careers, including information about sources of more expert advice on specific questions; making relevant records and reports;

66.2.3 making records of and reports on the personal and social needs of pupils;

66.2.4 communicating and consulting with the parents of pupils;

66.2.5 communicating and co-operating with persons or bodies outside the school; and

66.2.6 participating in meetings arranged for any of the purposes described above;

66.3 **Assessments and reports:**

providing or contributing to oral and written assessments, reports and references relating to individual pupils and groups of pupils;

66.4 **Appraisal:**

participating in arrangements made in accordance with regulations made under section 49 of the Education (No. 2) Act 1986 for the appraisal of his performance and that of other teachers;

66.5 **Review, induction, further training and development:**

66.5.1 reviewing from time to time his methods of teaching and programmes of work;

66.5.2 participating in arrangements for his further training and professional development as a teacher;

66.5.3 in the case of a teacher serving an induction period pursuant to the Induction Regulations, participating in arrangements for his supervision and training;

66.6 **Educational methods:**

advising and co-operating with the head teacher and other teachers (or any one or more of them) on the preparation and development of courses of study, teaching materials, teaching programmes, methods of teaching and assessment and pastoral arrangements;

66.7 **Discipline, health and safety:**

maintaining good order and discipline among the pupils and safeguarding their health and safety both when they are authorised to be on the school premises and when they are engaged in authorised school activities else where;

66.8 **Staff meetings:**

participating in meetings at the school which relate to the curriculum for the school or the administration or organisation of the school, including pastoral arrangements;

66.9 **Cover:**

69.9.1 subject to paragraph 66.9.2, supervising and so far as practicable teaching any pupils whose teacher is not available to teach them: subject to the exceptions in paragraph

66.9.3, **no teacher shall be required to provide such cover:**

(a) after the teacher who is absent or otherwise not available has been so for three or more consecutive working days; or

(b) where the fact that the teacher would be absent or otherwise not available for a period exceeding three consecutive working days was known to the maintaining authority or, in the case of a school which has a delegated budget, to the governing body, for two or more working days before the absence commenced;

66.9.3 **the exceptions are:**

(a) he is a teacher employed wholly or mainly for the purpose of providing such cover ("a supply teacher"); or

(b) the authority or the governing body (as the case may be) have exhausted all reasonable means of providing a supply teacher to provide cover without success; or

(c) he is a full-time teacher at the school but has been assigned by the head teacher in the time-table to teach or carry out other specified duties (except cover) for less than 75 per cent of those hours in the week during which pupils are taught at the school;

66.10   **Public examinations:**
(a) participating in arrangements for preparing pupils for public examinations
(b) and in assessing pupils for the purposes of such examinations; recording
(c) and reporting such assessments; and participating in arrangements for pupils' presentation for and supervision during such examinations;

66.11   **Management:**

66.11.1   contributing to the selection for appointment and professional development of other teachers and non-teaching staff, including the induction and assessment of new teachers and teachers serving induction periods pursuant to the Induction Regulations;

66.11.2   assisting the head teacher or an assessor in carrying out threshold assessments of other teachers for whom he has management responsibility;

66.11.3   co-ordinating the work of other teachers; and

66.11.4   taking such part as may be required of him in the review, development and management of activities relating to the curriculum, organisation and pastoral functions of the school;

66.12   **Administration:**

66.12.1   participating in administrative and organisational tasks related to such duties as are described above, including the management or supervision of persons providing support for the teachers in the school and the ordering and allocation of equipment and materials; and

66.12.2   attending assemblies, registering the attendance of pupils and supervising pupils, whether these duties are to be performed before, during or after school sessions.

Working time

67.1   The provisions of this paragraph shall not apply to deputy head teachers, assistant head teachers, advanced skills teachers, fast track teachers or to teachers employed to teach part-time and are subject to paragraphs 42.6, 43.2 and 43.3

67.2   A teacher employed full-time, other than in the circumstances described in paragraph 67.4, shall be available for work for 195 days in any school year, of which 190 days shall be days on which he may be required to teach pupils in addition to carrying out other duties; and those 195 days shall be specified by his employer or, if the employer so directs, by the head teacher.

67.3   Such a teacher shall be available to perform such duties at such times and such places as may be specified by the head teacher (or, where the teacher is not assigned to any one school, by his employer or the head teacher of any school in which he may for the time being be required to work as a teacher) for 1265 hours in any school year, those hours to be allocated reasonably throughout those days in the school year on which he is required to be available for work.

67.4   Paragraph 67.2 does not apply to such a teacher employed wholly or mainly to teach or perform other duties in relation to pupils in a residential establishment.

67.5   Time spent in travelling to or from the place of work shall not count against the 1265 hours referred to in paragraph 67.3.

67.6   Such a teacher shall not be required under his contract as a teacher to undertake midday supervision, and shall be allowed a break of reasonable length either between school sessions or between the hours of 12 noon and 2.00pm.

67.7   Such a teacher shall, in addition to the requirements set out in paragraphs 67.2 and 67.3, work such additional hours as may be needed to enable him to discharge effectively his professional duties, including, in particular, the marking of pupils' work, the writing of reports on pupils and the preparation of lessons, teaching material and teaching programmes. The amount of time required for this purpose beyond the 1265 hours referred to in paragraph 67.3 and the times outside the 1265 specified hours at which duties shall be performed shall not be defined by the employer but shall depend upon the work needed to discharge the teacher's duties.

Although it is highly unlikely that a Newly Qualified Teacher would be entering the teaching profession as an Advanced Skills Teacher, it is just possible that a mature entrant possessing exceptional qualifications could be appointed to such a position in a school. Furthermore, some of the Newly Qualified Teachers who are entering the teaching profession are on the Fast Track Teachers scheme. Although the Conditions of Employment for Advanced Skills Teachers and Fast Track Teachers are very similar (particularly those for Fast Track Teachers) to those of teachers other than head teachers (described in Part XII above), the short Section XI of the School Teachers' Pay and Conditions Document 2002 is reproduced below as this may be helpful for some of the readers of this booklet.

Part XI - Conditions of Employment of Advanced Skills Teachers and Fast Track Teachers

Professional duties

67.1   A teacher who is an advanced skills teacher, in addition to carrying out the professional duties of a teacher other than a head teacher (as described in Part XII) including those duties particularly assigned to him by the head teacher, may be required to carry out the following professional duties:

(a) participating in initial teacher training;

(b) participating in the induction and mentoring of newly qualified teachers;

(c) advising other teachers on classroom organisation and teaching methods;

(d) producing high quality teaching materials;

(e) disseminating to other teachers materials relating to best practice and educational research;

(f) advising on the provision of continuous professional development;

(g) participating in the appraisal of other teachers;

(h) helping teachers who are experiencing difficulties;

(i) producing high quality resources and materials, including video recordings of lessons, for dissemination in their own school and other schools.

61.2   An advanced skills teacher shall normally spend 20% of their time undertaking outreach work carrying out the duties in paragraph 61.1 with or for the benefit of teachers or trainee teachers from other schools, whether at the school of the advanced skills teacher, at that of the other teacher, in higher education institutions, at facilities of the authority or elsewhere.

62.   Subject to paragraph 67.1, the professional duties of a fast track teacher shall be the professional duties of a teacher other than a head teacher (as described in Part XII).

Daily break

63.   An advanced skills teacher or a fast track teacher shall be entitled to a break of reasonable length as near to the middle of each school day as is reasonably practicable.

3. The Sex Discrimination Act 1975 and the Equal Pay Act 1970

The Sex Discrimination Act 1975 renders unlawful (a) certain kinds of sex discrimination and (b) discrimination on the ground of marriage. Like race and disability discrimination, sex discrimination can be either **direct** or **indirect** and, in the definition of discrimination in this Act (the following paragraph), (a) is direct discrimination and (b) is indirect discrimination. The Act states:

1.- (1) A person discriminates against a woman in any circumstances relevant for the purposes of any provision of this Act if -

(a) on the ground of her sex he treats her less favourably than he treats, or would treat, a man; or

(b) he applies to her a requirement or condition which he applies or would apply equally to a man but -

(i) which is such that the proportion of women who can comply with it is considerably smaller than the proportion of men who can comply with it, and

(ii) which he cannot show to be justifiable irrespective of the sex of the person to whom it is applied, and

(iii) which is to her detriment because she cannot comply with it.

(2) If a person treats or would treat a man differently according to the man's marital status, his treatment of a woman is for the purposes of subsection 1(a) to be compared to his treatment of a man having the like marital status.

It is essential to note the very important fact that, although throughout the Sex Discrimination Act 1975 the term "woman" is used, sex discrimination against men is also unlawful under the Act and that *the provisions of Section*

1 relating to sex discrimination against women are to be read as applying equally to the treatment of men.

The Sex Discrimination Act protects all those applying for jobs. The Act states:

6.-(1) It is unlawful for a person, in relation to employment by him at an establishment in Great Britain, to discriminate against a woman –

(a) in the arrangements he makes for the purpose of determining who should be offered that employment; or

(b) on the terms on which he offers her that employment; or

(c) by refusing or deliberately omitting to offer her that employment.

Remembering that the Sex Discrimination Act 1975 applies to both women and men, this means that schools cannot, for example, normally advertise for a "headmistress" or a "schoolmaster". However, it is lawful to discriminate if the sex (or race) of the person is a genuine occupational qualification – although these are not common. In Part II of the Act, reasons why being a man or woman is a genuine occupational qualification are given. These include: physiology, the need to preserve decency or privacy, the nature of any living premises, the nature of the establishment – such as a hospital or prison, etc. Thus, depending upon the particular circumstances, a single sex boarding school that requires a male or a female resident teacher may well meet the genuine occupational qualification requirements of the Act. Furthermore, in a January 1998 BBC Radio 4 interview, a retired male head teacher stated that the Equal Opportunities Commission had allowed him to advertise for a male teacher who (when appointed) would be the only man on the staff other than the head teacher, on the grounds of the need to preserve privacy in supervising boys when they were changing for physical education.

Once employment has been obtained, the Act states:

6.- (2) It is unlawful for a person, in the case of a woman employed by him at an establishment in Great Britain, to discriminate against her –

(a) in the way he affords her access to opportunities for promotion, transfer or training, or to any other benefits, facilities or services, or by refusing or deliberately omitting to afford her access to them; or

(b) by dismissing her, or subjecting her to any other detriment.

Although sex discrimination cases frequently concern women, men also have rights under the Sex Discrimination Act as the 1998 *ACAS -v- Taylor* case demonstrates. Under the Act's provisions, Mr Taylor complained of unlawful sex discrimination in relation to a failure of ACAS (his employer) to promote him. The Employment Tribunal held that Mr Taylor had been unlawfully discriminated against by ACAS on the grounds that : (a) he had been treated less favourably than the other relevant female candidates; (b) ACAS's explanation for this was inadequate and unsatisfactory; and (c) the inference to be drawn was that a policy of positive discrimination toward women had been applied by ACAS.

It should be noted that the Sex Discrimination Act 1975 repealed and amended sections of the Equal Pay Act 1970. The Equal Pay Act's purpose is *to prevent discrimination, as regards terms and conditions of employment, between men and women* and, since 1975, there has been a statutory requirement to pay men and women equal pay for similar work. Although there have been a single salary scale for teachers (irrespective of whether they are male or female) in maintained schools for many years, there is some potential for unequal pay in respect of the actual point on the scale at which men and women are appointed. Although an employer has some discretion as to where on the salary scale a person should be placed, this must reflect criteria – such as ability, skills and experience. Whereas teachers' salaries are often paid by local education authorities, the levels of salary paid to teachers are generally set by school governors. If disparity in pay emerges between sexes at different schools, then a complaint may be made to an Employment Tribunal. If the complaint is upheld, then the pay inequalities must be remedied. A Scottish example of this was *South Ayrshire Council -v- Morton (2000)* where a court permitted comparison between the pay of teachers in two different local education authorities. This, combined with the existence of a national pay scale, provided a reasonable basis for comparison of the teachers' salaries.

Furthermore, if appropriate, a case can be taken against an individual employer (which it could be in, say, the case of an independent school). For example, in the case of *Benneviste -v- University of Southampton (1989)*, Dr Benneviste was appointed as a lecturer but at a salary level which was below normal for a person of her experience and age and so she claimed equal pay with four male lecturing colleagues who were doing the same work. The case eventually went to the Court of Appeal which decided that, as Dr Benneviste's contract was less favourable than the contracts of her male colleagues and that she was being paid less than they were for the same work, she was entitled to equal pay.

It should also be noted that, in October 1999, two women won a landmark test case for all women claiming arrears of pay when they have been paid less than men doing the same or equivalent jobs. The Employment Appeal Tribunal in London ruled that the two-year limit on the amount of back pay that could be recovered was in breach of European law and that women should be allowed to claim arrears going back six years from the time that a claim is launched. This ruling, unless overturned in the Court of Appeal, means that providing they have been in the job long enough, the amount of back pay that can be recovered by an employee has trebled.

The Sex Discrimination Act 1975 also contains provisions protecting pregnant employees. Providing she has fulfilled the qualifying period with her employer, a woman has a basic statutory employment right to maternity leave and to return to work after her maternity leave. She has the right to return to the job she was doing beforehand, with the same terms and conditions, and is entitled to any pay rises implemented during her maternity leave period. However, some women decide that they would prefer to return to part-time or job-share work (rather than full-time work) on the completion of their maternity leave. Although there is no statutory right to return to work on a part-time or job-share basis, if a woman worked full-time prior to her maternity, a refusal by an employer to allow such a return could well be challenged as indirect sex discrimination. Refusal to allow a woman to return to work on a part-time or job-share basis is, under Clause (1)(b)(i) of the Sex Discrimination Act 1975, now regarded as a requirement or condition being applied.

Courts and Employment Tribunals now recognise that the greater burden in the raising of children, with its implications for full-time employment, rests with women rather than men and, therefore, women are less able to work full-time than men. If, following maternity leave, a woman's request to return to work on a part-time or job share basis is refused, the employer should provide detailed and specific reasons why the arrangement would not work. If a teacher believes that she has been discriminated against in this way, then she should contact the legal department of her union immediately because claims for sex discrimination must be lodged at an Employment Tribunal within three months of the act that is the subject of the complaint and this period begins when the head teacher, or the school's governing body, refuses the teacher's request.

Furthermore, married employees have additional protection under the Act. In terms of discrimination against a married person under the Sex Discrimination Act 1975, the Act states:

3.-(1) A person discriminates against a married person of either sex in any circumstances relevant for the purposes of any provision of Part II [discrimination in the field of employment] if -

(a) on the ground of his or her marital status he treats that person less favourably than he treats or would treat an unmarried person of the same sex, or

(b) he applies to that person a requirement or condition which he applies or would apply equally to an unmarried person but -

> (i) which is such that the proportion of married persons who can comply with it is considerably smaller than the proportion of unmarried persons of the same sex who can comply with it, and
>
> (ii) which he cannot show to be justifiable irrespective of the marital status of the person to whom it is applied, and
>
> (iii) which is to that person's detriment because he cannot comply with it.

Discrimination against a married person can be either direct or indirect; in the above paragraph (a) is direct discrimination and (b) is indirect discrimination.

Furthermore, if someone brings proceedings against a discriminator, gives evidence or information in connection with discrimination proceedings, or alleges discrimination, they are given protection from victimisation by the discriminator. The Sex Discrimination Act 1975 defines what this means:

4.- (1) A person ("the discriminator") discriminates against another person ("the person victimised") in any circumstances relevant for the purposes of this Act if he treats the person victimised less favourably than in those circumstances he treats or would treat, other persons ...".

It is also important to note that, in *MacDonald –v- Ministry of Defence (2000)*, an Employment Appeal Tribunal (EAT) overturned twenty-five years of legal opinion and rulings that **sexual orientation** was not covered by the Sex Discrimination Act 1975. Roderick MacDonald was a homosexual member of staff at the Ministry of Defence until he was forced to resign and he took his case to tribunal on the basis of sex discrimination and sexual harassment. The Employment Tribunal Chairman concluded that, under the Sex Discrimination Act 1975, "sex" had two possible meanings – "gender" and "orientation". (The Chairman also made use of the European Convention on Human Rights (to which the United Kingdom is a signatory); the European Court of Human Rights held that sexual orientation is included under the Convention and therefore the United Kingdom is bound by this.) The Employment Appeal Tribunal concluded that the appropriate comparison to make when considering such a case of sex discrimination was not between the treatment of a gay man and a lesbian (since the treatment of a lesbian might be equally bad) but, rather, between a gay man and a heterosexual woman. When making such a comparison, any differences demonstrated could well show the existence of sex discrimination. Clearly this benchmark ruling on sexual orientation is important in employment.

In addition it should also be noted that, resulting from a European Court of Justice case (*P -v- S and Cornwall County Council 1996)* the Sex Discrimination (Gender Reassignment) Regulations 1999 extended the Sex Discrimination Act 1975 to cover sex discrimination in employment on the grounds of **gender reassignment**. Discrimination on the grounds of transsexuality in the area of recruitment is now unlawful (except where a Genuine Occupational Qualification applies) and protection for employees is now provided against discrimination by employers at all stages of a gender reassignment process.

The Sex Discrimination Act 1975 clearly provides both employees and those seeking employment with considerable protection. If any teacher believes that he/she has been discriminated against on grounds of their sex, their sexual orientation, or their marital status, then he/she should always seek professional advice from the legal department of their union as quickly as possible.

Finally, it is worth mentioning the fact that, under the Sex Discrimination Act 1975, an employer can insist on a particular **dress code**. Therefore, a head teacher could legally impose a code that (for example) stipulated shirts and ties for male teachers and skirts and blouses for female teachers. The leading case here is *Schmidt –v- Austwicks Bookshops (1977)*, where the bookshop had a dress code that its female staff could not wear trousers and had to wear skirts. Miss Schmidt claimed that her employer's refusal to let her wear trousers (which the male staff had to wear) was unlawful sex discrimination under the Sex Discrimination Act 1975. Miss Schmidt lost her case. The Employment Appeal Tribunal ruled that an employer was entitled to a wide discretion in controlling the image of their establishment and that although there were similar, although different, rules for male staff, no unlawful sex discrimination arose. Furthermore, more recent cases (for example, a Court of Appeal case where a supermarket employee who was dismissed for refusing to cut his long pony tail) have confirmed the *Schmidt –v- Austwicks Bookshops (1977)* ruling. Therefore, it is legitimate under the Sex Discrimination Act 1975 for an employer to enforce a policy of smart and/or conventional dress appearance – even if there are different rules for men and women – providing that, taken as a whole, neither gender is treated less favourably. However, it is important to note that, under race discrimination legislation, rules on dress (including the wearing of headgear and/or skirts) must be applied carefully and sympathetically

4. The Race Relations Act 1976, the Race Relations (amendment) Act 2000, and the Commission for Racial Equality's "Code of Conduct for the Elimination of Racial Discrimination in Employment"

The Race Relations Act 1976 is concerned with (a) discrimination on racial grounds and (b) relations between people of different racial groups. Racial discrimination can be either **direct** or **indirect** and, in the definition of discrimination in the Act (the following paragraph), (a) is direct discrimination and (b) is indirect discrimination. The Act states:

1.- (1) A person discriminates against another in any circumstances relevant for the purposes of any provision of this Act if –
(a) on racial grounds he treats that other less favourably than he treats or would treat other persons; or
(b) he applies to that other a requirement or condition which he applies or would apply equally to persons not of the same racial group as that other, but –
   (i) which is such that the proportion of persons of the same racial group as that other who can comply with it is considerably smaller than the proportion of persons not of that racial group who can comply with it; and
   (ii) which he cannot show to be justifiable irrespective of the colour, race, nationality or ethnic or national origins of the person to whom it is applied; and
   (iii) which is to the detriment of that other person because he cannot comply with it.
(2)   It is hereby declared that, for the purposes of this Act, segregating a person from other persons on racial grounds is treating him less favourably than they are treated.

The Act defines the terms "racial grounds" and "racial group":

3.- (1) In this Act, unless the context otherwise requires –

"racial grounds" means any of the following grounds, namely colour, race, nationality or ethnic or national origins;
"racial group" means a group of persons defined by reference to colour, race, nationality or ethnic or national origins, and references to a person's racial group refer to any racial group into which he falls.

The Race Relations Act 1976 protects those seeking jobs. The Act states:

4.- (1) It is unlawful for a person, in relation to employment by him at an establishment in Great Britain, to discriminate against another -
(a) in the arrangements he makes for the purpose of determining who should be offered that employment; or
(b) in the terms on which he offers him that employment; or by refusing or deliberately omitting to offer him that employment.

However, it must be noted that (with the specific exception of Northern Ireland) discrimination may be lawful on religious grounds and schools with a religious foundation may advertise for a teacher belonging to a particular faith.

Once employment has been obtained, the Race Relations Act 1976 provides employees with protection from racial discrimination. The Act states:

4.- (2) It is unlawful for a person, in the case of a person employed by him at an establishment in Great Britain, to discriminate against that employee -
(a) in the terms of employment which he affords him; or
(b) in the way he affords him access to opportunities for promotion, transfer or training, or to any other benefits, facilities or services, or by refusing or deliberately omitting to afford him access to them; or by dismissing him, or subjecting him to any other detriment.

This is illustrated in the case of *Quereshi, –v– University of Manchester (1997)*. Here the Industrial Tribunal (now known as an Employment Tribunal) which heard the case decided that Dr Quereshi (a law lecturer at the University) had been both unlawfully discriminated against and victimised on racial grounds with regard to his promotion applications and in the way that his complaints were dealt with. He was awarded substantial "damages with interest" against both the University and the head of his faculty. The Tribunal strongly commented that, "the University should proceed speedily to adopt and implement effective equal opportunities policies which are understood and practised by those considering persons for appointment and promotion".

As the above example shows, racial discrimination can also be by way of victimisation and the Race Relations Act 1976 states,.

2.- (1) A person ("the discriminator") discriminates against another person ("the person victimised") in any circumstances relevant for the purposes of any provision of this Act if he treats the person victimised less favourably than in those circumstances he treats or would treat other persons, ...

Therefore, the Race Relations Act 1976 provides both employees and those seeking employment with considerable protection. If any teacher believes that he/she has been discriminated against on racial grounds or as a member of a particular racial group, then he/she should always seek professional advice from the legal department of their union as quickly as possible.

The Stephen Lawrence enquiry *("to enquire into the matters arising from the death of Stephen Lawrence")* was set up in July 1997 and the Inquiry Report was published in February 1999. In the Report it stated that, *"if racism is to be eliminated from our society there must be a co-ordinated effort to prevent its growth ... it is incumbent upon every institution to examine their policies and practices to guard against disadvantaging any section of our community."* The government, in its response, went considerably further than the Inquiry Report suggested and it extended and amended the Race Relations Act 1976 through the means of the Race Relations (Amendment) Act 2000.

The Race Relations (Amendment) Act 2000 extended protection against racial discrimination by "specified public authorities", and these include the governing bodies of educational establishments maintained by local education authorities. There is now a general obligatory duty requiring all specified public authorities to promote race equality. In everything they do, the specified public authorities have a general statutory duty:

(a)   to eliminate unlawful racial discrimination; *and*
(b)   to promote equality of opportunity good relations between persons of different racial groups.

The Commission for Racial Equality is issuing six Codes of Practice, one specifically for educational bodies. Furthermore, in Chapter 6, paragraph 16 of a document from the Home Office discussing the Race Relations (Amendment) Act 2000, it stated (2001):

... we are proposing that each school in England and Wales should have specific duties to:

(a)   prepare a **written policy** on race equality;

(b)   **assess** the impact of its policies on ethnic minority pupils, staff and parents, with the emphasis on the attainment of ethnic minority pupils;

(c)   **monitor** the levels of attainment of ethnic minority pupils, and the impact of the its race equality policy on pupils, staff and parents.

Quite clearly, whilst the overall emphasis is on pupils, it is quite clear that there are aspects which apply to school staff. Schools will each have to assess and monitor the impact of their race equality policies in regards to their staff. From now on, all schools will have to consider their race policies very carefully and, in many cases, be more pro-active regarding maters of race than they have might been in the past.

The Commission for Racial Equality's 1984 publication *"Code of Practice for the elimination of racial discrimination and the promotion of equality of opportunity in employment"* was produced before the Race Relations (Amendment) Act 2002 was passed. (The Commission for Racial Equality states that guidelines on implementing the general duty specified in the Race Relations (Amendment) Act 2000 will be available in due course.) However, notwithstanding the fact that the *"Code of Practice for the elimination of racial discrimination and the promotion of equality of opportunity in employment"* was produced before the Race Relations (Amendment) Act 2002 was passed, it nevertheless contains extremely helpful information and guidance.

The Code's purpose is *"to give practical guidance which will help employers, trade unions, employment agencies and employees to understand not only the provisions of the Race Relations Act (1976) and their implications, but also how best they can implement policies to eliminate racial discrimination and to enhance equality of opportunity".*

The Code states its purpose and its status and proceeds first to outline the responsibilities of employers. These include: the employer's equal opportunity policy; the recruitment and selection process; the treatment of applicants; terms of employment; training and transfers; performance appraisals; grievance and disciplinary procedures; dismissal procedures;

cultural and religious needs; etc.

The Code next outlines the responsibilities of individual employees. It makes it quite clear that, "*While the primary responsibility for providing equal opportunity rests with the employer, individual employees at all levels and of all racial groups have responsibilities too. Good race relations depend on them as much as on management, and so their attitudes and activities are very important.*" The Code outlines the actions that would be unlawful by individual employees under the Race Relations Act 1976 and recommends that individual employees, to assist in promoting equal opportunity and preventing racial discrimination, should: (a) co-operate in measures introduced by management designed to ensure equal opportunity and non-discrimination; (b) where such measures have not been introduced, press for their introduction; (c) draw the attention of management and (where appropriate) their union to suspected discriminatory acts or practices; and (d) refrain from harassment or intimidation of other employees on racial grounds. The Code concludes by discussing briefly the responsibilities of trade unions and employment agencies.

It is clear that as employees, individual teachers have responsibilities under the race relations legislation. Furthermore, if they are in a management position (such as a Head of Department or member of the Leadership Group) they also have responsibilities that interact with the responsibilities of the employer. In addition (as the section of this booklet which covers inclusion and discrimination shows) teachers must take care to ensure that their treatment of pupils is always non-discriminatory. This can be complex and teachers must always ensure that both their behaviour and their actions are professional and within the law.

5. The Disability Discrimination Act 1995 and DfEE Circular 3/97 "What the Disability Discrimination Act (DDA) 1995 means for Schools and LEAs"

The Disability Discrimination Act 1995 created rights for disabled people and it is largely (although not entirely) aimed at preventing discrimination against disabled employees. The Act made it unlawful to discriminate against disabled people in employment (and in the provision of goods and services to disabled people). However, unlike both the Sex Discrimination Act 1975 and the Race Relations Act 1976, which cover direct and indirect discrimination, the Disability Discrimination Act 1995 only covers direct discrimination.

The Disability Rights Commission, the organisation with overall responsibility for the provisions of the Disability Discrimination Act 1995, has three main functions: (1) to work towards the elimination of discrimination against disabled people; (2) to promote the equalisation of opportunities for disabled people; and (3) to keep under review the working of the disability discrimination legislation.

It must be made absolutely clear that only someone who meets the stringent definition of a disabled person can enjoy the rights that this Act confers. Section 1(1) of the Disability Discrimination Act 1995 defines a disabled person as someone who has "*a physical or mental impairment which has a substantial and long-term adverse effect on his ability to carry out normal day-to-day activities*". (An individual can have a physical or mental impairment that has a substantial and long-term effect but still not qualify for the protection of the Act unless they can show that their disability substantially affects their normal day-to-day activities.) A medical assessment is, almost always, likely to be necessary, and long-term means that the disability must have lasted, or can be expected to last, for at least twelve months.

The employment provisions contained in Part II of the Disability Discrimination Act 1995 came into force in December 1996 and DfEE

Circular 3/97 provides guidance on the implications of the Act for both local education authorities and schools in England. Because the Act's employment provisions do not now apply to employers with fewer than fifteen employees, some very small voluntary-aided or independent preparatory schools may, therefore, be exempt. However, all local education authority maintained schools, regardless of their size, are covered by the DDA because the local education authority is the employer, not the school. The DfEE 3/97 Circular states the main employment provisions of the Disability Discrimination Act 1995 mean that:

(a)   employers must not unjustifiably discriminate against current or prospective employees with disabilities, or those who have had disabilities in the past. This applies to every aspect of work including recruitment, terms & conditions of service, promotion, training and the dismissal process. The Act does not prevent an employer from appointing the best person for the job ; and

(b)   employers may have to make reasonable adjustments to their employment arrangements or premises if these sub- stantially disadvantage a disabled employee compared to a non-disabled person. For prospective employees they must investigate whether there is any reasonable adjustment which would overcome a disadvantage to a disabled applicant before deciding if they are the most suitable person for the job.

DfEE Circular 3/97 gives examples of reasonable adjustments which gov- erning bodies and local education authorities might consider making. These are: altering premises; allocating some duties to another employee; transferring the person to fill an existing vacancy; altering working hours; changing the person's place of work; allowing absences during working hours for rehabilitation, assessment or treatment; supplying additional training; acquiring or making changes to equipment; and providing a reader or a signer. There are no fixed rules; each case needs to be consid- ered carefully in the light of the disabled person's needs. Furthermore, the Circular also discusses how Employment Tribunals decide whether an adjustment is "reasonable". This involves such factors as: how much alter- ation is necessary, ease of making the adjustment; and how much this will all cost together within the employer's overall resources.

The crux of the case of *Humphreys –v- Environment Agency (1999)* concerned "reasonable adjustments". Here a disabled employee was transferred from her post to a lower graded position while the employer attempted to find alternative work for her in her own grade; however, although posts were identified, they were all declined. The Employment Appeal Tribunal stated that this was the extent of the employer's obligations. Thus, whilst an employer is required to make "reasonable adjustments", these do not amount to treating an employee more favourably and do not oblige an employer to dismiss other employees in order to accommodate a disabled employee.

If, in the course of their employment, teachers become disabled, they should discuss, with their employer, whether reasonable adjustments can be made so that they can continue in post. If this proves to be difficult, then they should always seek professional advice from their union as quickly as possible.

In order to show that (under the provisions of the Disability Discrimination Act 1995) discrimination has taken place, it is important to ensure that the following three points can all be proven: (1) that the employer treated the person with a disability less favourably than someone without that disability; (2) that the reason for that treatment related to that disability; and (3) that the treatment could not be justified by the employer. Unless all three points can be proven it is unlikely that a disability discrimination case would prove to be successful at an Employment Tribunal.

If a disabled prospective employee believes that an employer has unlawfully discriminated against them, or has refused to consider making reasonable adjustments, then they have the right to complain to an Employment Tribunal. However, it must be noted that there are particular circumstances where a less favourable treatment of a disabled prospective employee (or an employee who become disabled in the course of their employment) may be justified. It should also be noted that government regulations state that no one who is medically unfit to teach should be employed as a teacher and the health, education and welfare of pupils are of paramount importance in reaching a medical decision on an individual's fitness to teach. If a disabled teacher is experiencing difficulty in obtaining a teaching post, then they would be wise to seek professional advice from a union.

Furthermore, under the Disability Discrimination Act 1995, (like sex and race discrimination), the law protects any person taking action, considering taking action, or alleging that someone has infringed the Act from victimisation.

The process for complaints under the Disability Discrimination Act 1995 is modelled on the procedures for sex and race discrimination and complaints must be brought to Employment Tribunals within three months of the date of the act complained of.

Finally, it is worth noting that the employment sections of the Disability Discrimination Act 1995 have been in force since December 1996 and there is now a substantial body of case law under the Act.

6. DfEE Circular 4/99 "Physical and Mental Fitness to Teach of Teachers and of Entrants to Initial Teacher Training"

DfEE Circular 4/99 provides guidance on the procedures for assessing the physical and mental fitness of both existing teachers and of those applying for teacher training courses. It explains the implications of Regulations 7 to 10A of the Teachers Regulations and the Disability Discrimination Act 1995, both of which are relevant to employing teachers. The Circular outlines the procedures for barring or restricting employment as a teacher on medical grounds and also offers guidance to medical advisers on medical standards.

The Circular states that a high standard of physical and mental health to enter and remain in the teaching profession is required because teaching is a demanding career and teachers have to act *in loco parentis* for the pupils in their charge. The health, education, safety and welfare of pupils are important in deciding on an individual's fitness to teach. Employers (and initial teacher training providers) not only need to assess the medical fitness of teachers seeking work, they must also be concerned with the continuing fitness of teachers in employment. If necessary, employers can take steps to suspend or terminate a teacher's employment on medical grounds. However, this is not to say that those with disabilities cannot become teachers or that a teacher who becomes disabled must automatically leave the teaching profession. In fact, at the present time, the Teacher Training Agency is making efforts to attract more people with disabilities into teaching because this sector of the population is under-represented in teaching. Many teachers who have, or develop, a disability are medically fit to teach although (as discussed in the last section) their employers may have to make reasonable adjustments under the Disability Discrimination Act 1995 to enable them to carry out their duties effectively (see DfEE Circular 3/97 *"What the Disability Discrimination Act 1995 means for Schools and LEAs).*

Regulations 8 and 9 of the Teachers' Regulations make it clear that a local education authority or governing body must not appoint anyone to, or continue to employ them in, relevant employment unless he or she has the health and physical capacity for such employment. However, every case must be treated individually.

Medical advisers must classify teachers (and intending teachers) into one of three categories A, B or C. DfEE Circular 4/99 describes each category:

(a)   Those who are in good health and free from conditions which might be likely to interfere with efficiency of teaching;

(b)   Those who are in generally good health but who suffer from conditions which are likely to interfere to some extent with their efficiency in teaching either all subjects or certain specified subjects, though these conditions are not serious enough to make the candidate unfit for the teaching profession. This includes those whose disability could require employers to make reasonable adjustment to enable them to provide effective and efficient teaching; or

(c)   Those whose condition is such to make them unfit for the teaching profession. Candidates should not normally be included in this category unless they have a psychiatric or physical disorder likely to interfere seriously with regular and efficient teaching of either general subjects or the subject in which they intend to specialise e.g. PE or science subjects, or if they have an illness which may carry a risk to the safety or welfare of the pupils.

Clearly, in the course of their employment, some teachers do, become unable to continue working because of injury or illness and, in such circumstances, they can apply for ill-health retirement benefits under the Teachers' Pension Scheme. (To qualify for ill-health benefits, a teacher has to be permanently incapable of teaching and a special team of medical advisers, appointed by the Department for Education and Skills, considers all applications for ill-health retirement benefits.) In most such cases of this type, a teacher's application for ill-health retirement benefits will have been initiated by the teacher (often with the help of their employer and sometimes with the help of their union).

However, the Regulations require employers to initiate emergency proceedings if they believe it necessary - usually when a governing body or a head teacher considers a teacher may have become medically incapable of performing teaching duties if this may put at risk the health, education, safety or welfare of pupils. Local education authorities and governing bodies have the power to suspend teachers where necessary. However, any such suspension should only be carried out on the advice of an appropriately qualified medical adviser (normally with competence in occupational medicine). In all circumstances where the issue of dismissal of a teacher on medical grounds arises, the teacher must be given the opportunity to submit medical and other evidence and to make representations, etc. In such circumstances, the teacher should consider taking professional advice from their medical practitioner and/or their union.

It is also important to note that the Secretary of State for Education and Skills has the power to make Directions barring a person on medical grounds from relevant employment (Regulation 10 of the Teachers' Regulations). However, DfEE Circular 4/99 states that "*broadly speaking, barring will only be considered in cases where a person is suffering from an illness that implies a risk or potential risk to the safety and welfare of pupils and colleagues. It is most likely to be considered for a person suffering from mental illness who has displayed psychotic or manic symptoms, and in cases of severe alcohol or drug misuse*".

DfES List 99 contains the details of all those people whose employment has been barred or restricted on either misconduct or medical grounds. However, those people barred on medical grounds are listed separately from those barred on misconduct grounds and, furthermore, no details of their illnesses are given.

7. The Health And Safety At Work Act 1974, Sections 7 & 8

The Health and Safety at Work Act 1974 is concerned with securing the health, safety and welfare of persons at work, for protecting others against risks to health or safety in connection with the activities of persons at work, for controlling the keeping and use and preventing the unlawful acquisition, possession and use of dangerous substances, and for controlling certain emissions into the atmosphere.

Although much of the Health and Safety at Work Act 1974 legislation is aimed at workplaces with obvious dangers (such as farms, quarries and factories), schools possess many potential danger areas (such as corridors, stairs, offices, classrooms, laboratories, canteens, halls/gymnasiums, playgrounds and sports fields) and must comply fully with the Act's provisions. Furthermore, it should be noted worth that one in twelve of the accidents reported to the Health and Safety Executive occur in education establishments. It is also important to note that teachers' responsibilities under the Health and Safety at Work Act are closely interrelated with their common law duty of care for their pupils (see this booklet's section on Protecting Children).

Employers can face criminal prosecution by the Health and Safety Executive for a breach of statutory care if they have not taken reasonable steps to protect an employee's health and "stress" falls within this area. In the case of *Walker –v- Northumberland County Council (1995)*, Mr Walker was awarded £170,000 for stress in his unacceptable working situation. In the case of *Morrall –v- Shropshire Education Authority (2000)*, Mr Morrall was awarded £300,000 because his employer had not addressed his very stressful working environment. Schools can be stressful working environments (some schools being very much worse than others) and it is, therefore, important (as these two cases demonstrate) to ensure that, if necessary, the teacher's employer takes all reasonable steps to reduce workplace stress.

Although much of the Health and Safety at Work Act 1974 is concerned with the duties of employers, and their responsibility for their employees, both Section 7 and Section 8 of the Act makes it clear that every employee in an organisation, right up to the highest level of management, also has personal responsibilities.

The general statutory duties of employees are stated in the Act:

7. It shall be the duty of every employee while at work _
    to take reasonable care for the health and safety of himself
    and of other persons who may be affected by his acts or omissions at work; and
    as regards any duty or requirement imposed on his employer,
    or any other person by or under any of the relevant statutory
    provisions, to co-operate with him so far as is necessary to
    enable that duty to be performed or complied with.

It should be noted that in (a) "other persons" includes members of the public and in (b) "any other person" could, in the case of a school, be the head teacher or the head of a department, etc.

Because Section 7 of the Health and Safety at Work Act 1974 places a personal responsibility for ensuring health and safety at work, **every employee has a statutory duty to report anything they believe is dangerous** (for example, a frayed flex on the staff room kettle or a hole in a corridor carpet) and it is wise to do this in writing and to keep a copy. Once the employee has formally reported the perceived danger they are absolved of responsibility and the employer has to consider the matter. If the employer does nothing then, should there be an accident, the employer might be found to be negligent. However, if an employee notices something dangerous and does not report it then, should an accident occur, the employee could be guilty of contributory negligence. Safety often costs money but both employers and employees should always remember the adage, "If you think safety is expensive, then try an accident" because a successful claim for damages can now run into many thousands of pounds.

Furthermore, Section 8 of the Health and Safety at Work Act 1974 states that employees have a duty not to interfere with or misuse anything that an employer has provided for safety purposes according to statutory requirements.

8. No person shall intentionally or recklessly interfere with or
    misuse anything provided in the interests of health, safety or
    welfare in pursuance of any of the relevant statutory provisions.

For example, when schools provide safety clothing (such as safety goggles for use in science lessons) or safety equipment (such as fire extinguishers), then they must not be misused and they must always be left in the correct locations.

As far as health and safety at work is concerned, there are certain implied (i.e. not stated) conditions in contracts of employment and, as far as individual employees are concerned, the two principal implied conditions are: (1) that employees will carry out all their duties with reasonable skill and not to be negligent; and (2) the duty of obedience or co-operation with an employer.

With respect to school teachers, the first implied condition has major implications. There is a clear duty for teachers to carry out all of their duties professionally and to take very great care to avoid getting into a situation where the safety of a pupil(s), or another member(s) of staff, could be in danger through any negligence on the teacher's part. If it is shown that a pupil(s), or others, have come to any harm because of a teacher's negligence, then the consequences for the teacher's future in the profession may be disastrous. For example, in April 2002, a teacher who led a school boating trip in 1999 on which a nine-year old schoolgirl died (when a motorboat carrying nine children from a Hampshire school capsized in Portsmouth Harbour), was sent to the Crown Court for sentencing after pleading guilty to failing to take adequate precautions of protecting the health and safety of the people in his care. (The school also pleaded guilty to one charge under the Health and Safety at Work Act 1974).

The Health and Safety at Work Act 1974 is now well over a quarter of a century old and there have been many amendments made to the 1974 legislation. Much recent health and safety at work legislation has been concerned with the **assessment of risk**. For example, the "Management of Health and Safety at Work Regulations 1992", requires employers to carry out an assessment of the risks to the health and safety of their staff whilst they are at work. Under Section 13A(1) of the Regulations, employers of women of child-bearing age (and a large, and increasing, number of teachers are women) must assess their jobs for particular risks relating to pregnancy. Risk assessments must be carried out on the job of any pregnant woman to identify any unacceptable risks associated with physical aspects (of the workplace), working conditions, working practices, and presence/absence of biological and/or chemical agents. If an unacceptable risk is identified, the employer must consider adjusting the working conditions or hours, or transferring the pregnant employee to other duties. If this is not possible then the woman must be suspended on full pay to avoid the risk.

However, employees also have risk assessment responsibilities, and this affects teachers. For example, if a teacher wishes to take a class off the school premises for a geography field trip, the teacher should always carry out a thorough assessment of any potential risks to both pupils and accompanying adults when planning the field trip. Unless this is done properly, and it can be shown that this was done properly, then both the teacher and their employer could find themselves in difficulty defending a charge of negligence if an accident occurs. Although pupils are not employees, teachers nevertheless have legal responsibilities for pupils whilst they are under their care. It is wise to remember that, as a society, we have now become very much more litigious.

It is very important to remember that accidents at work do happen occasionally and teachers sometimes sustain injuries whilst they are at work. Employers are required to keep Accident Books and report certain injuries (such as some types of fracture and eye injuries) to the Health and Safety Executive under The Reporting of Injuries, Diseases and Dangerous Occurrences Regulations 1985. If an accident occurs to an employee, it is very important to ensure that a formal entry is made in the Accident Book. Unless this is done, it can be difficult, at a later date, to prove when an accident took place. It is also wise to enter details in the Accident Book of any accident that happens to a pupil(s), including any accidents which occur off the school premises when the pupils are under a teacher's formal supervision. (Schools should have a set procedure for this.)

Finally, if in the course of employment, an employee sustains an injury, the employee may be able to claim Industrial Injuries Benefit (or other benefits) from the Benefits Agency. Although employers should advise employees who have suffered injury at work, this is not always the case. In the case of any serious injury or permanent/semi-permanent disability caused by an accident at work, it is sensible to seek professional advice from their union at the earliest opportunity. In claiming benefits, delays could result in the benefit (or part of it) being lost.

8. DfEE Guidance Note 10/9/98 "Recruitment and Selection Procedures: Vetting Teachers and Other Staff who will have Contact with Children", the Criminal Records Bureau, Misconduct of Teachers, and the Sexual Offences (Amendment) Act 2000

The DfEE Guidance Note 10/9/98 *"Recruitment and Selection Procedures: Vetting Teachers and Other Staff who will have Contact with Children"* was produced because there had been considerable publicity concerning a case in which a teacher made wholly false claims about his academic qualifications. The DfEE guidance suggested that local education authorities, schools, other educational institutions, and teacher employment agencies should review their selection and appointment procedures to ensure that appropriate checks were made on people selected for appointment. (Another helpful DfEE document is the DfEE's October 2000 Guidance for Education Staff leaflet titled *"Preventing Unsuitable People from Working with Children and Young Persons"*).

At that time, the standard checks were: Identity, List 99 (to see if the candidate was barred from employment by the Secretary of State), Qualified Teacher Status, Health, Criminal Background, Academic Qualifications, Previous Employment History, and Professional and Character References. Some of these checks were mandatory (such as the List 99 check) whilst some were strongly advised as good practice in order to guard against false claims and/or deception, (Serious, deliberate, fraud or deception in connection with an application for employment may amount to a criminal offence – "Obtaining Pecuniary Advantage by Deception".) Although some checks (such as the mandatory health check to ascertain physical and mental fitness to teach) remain the responsibility of the employer (or the initial teacher training institution), DfEE Guidance Note of 10/9/1998 has been discontinued. The reason for this is probably because the Criminal Records Bureau now undertakes many of the checks listed in the DfEE Guidance Note of 10/9/1998.

The Criminal Records Bureau was established under the Police Act 1997 to improve the criminal record checks system and, thus, provide better protection for children (and other vulnerable people) from those who might wish to harm them. Employers use the Criminal Records Bureau's Disclosure service to help establish if a successful candidate has a background that may make him or her unsuitable for the job, or voluntary position, in question. The Bureau utilises four primary sources of information: (1) the Police National Computer (the centralised information point for the police forces of England and Wales); (2) local police force records (which includes relevant non-conviction information); (3) the Department for Education and Skills' List 99 which lists data on people who are considered unsuitable for work with children (or vulnerable adults); and (4) similar records held by the Department of Health (which, like the DfES, also holds a list of people considered unsuitable to work with children).

The Criminal Records Bureau provides three levels of checks: Enhanced, Standard, and Basic. The Enhanced Level check is intended for teachers and teachers in training (as well as others who work in schools, such as school caretakers or school governors). Enhanced Disclosure shows all convictions a person has incurred, including spent convictions, cautions, reprimands, and bind-overs. Every time teachers obtain a new post resulting in a change of local education authority, they must undergo and complete satisfactorily the Criminal Records Bureau's Enhanced Disclosure procedure before they can commence duties in their new school.

Requirement R1.5 of the DfES/TTA "Requirements for Initial Teacher Training" 2002 stipulates that "All providers must ensure that systems are in place to seek information on whether entrants have a criminal background which might prevent them working with children or young persons, or as a teacher, and ensure that entrants have not been previously excluded from teaching and working with children." All initial teacher training students must now undergo and complete the Criminal Records Bureau's Enhanced Disclosure procedure satisfactorily before they can commence their school placements.

As far as the statutory criminal background check for teachers is concerned, all past convictions, bind-over orders or cautions **must** be disclosed. (Normally, under the provisions of The Rehabilitation of Offenders Act 1974, convictions which are "spent" under the terms of the Act need not be disclosed).

Since 1995, automatic barring has resulted where anyone who is, has been, or is seeking to become employed in "relevant employment" (which includes teaching), is found guilty, or pleads guilty to, a sexual offence which involves a child under sixteen years of age. (The sexual offences or attempted sexual offences include: rape, buggery, incest, unlawful sexual intercourse, indecent assault, gross indecency, and taking or distributing indecent photographs.) It is highly unlikely that anyone who has been convicted of one of these offences would ever be permitted to teach in a school. If a practising school teacher is convicted of one of these offences then - as well as being dismissed from their position, probably being given a custodial sentence and placed on the Sexual Offenders' Register - they will also be placed on DfES List 99.

The sexual offences listed above lead to automatic barring by the Secretary of State but there are other offences where, although the Secretary of State has the power to bar a person for misconduct, the Secretary of State is not obliged to do so. However, the following offences are very likely to lead to a bar or a restriction being imposed on the teacher: violent behaviour towards people or young people; a sexual, or otherwise inappropriate, relationship with a pupil (regardless of whether the pupil is over the legal age of consent); a sexual offence against someone over the age of sixteen; any offence involving serious violence; drug trafficking and other drug related offences; stealing school property or monies; deception in relation to employment as a teacher or at a school (such as false claims about qualifications or failure to disclose past convictions); any conviction which results in a custodial sentence of more than twelve month's imprisonment; and repeated misconduct or multiple convictions, unless of a very minor nature. However, it is important to note that this list is by no means exhaustive.

It is important to point out that the Sexual Offences (Amendment) Act 2000 is also legislation that, as employees, teachers must comply with. The Sexual Offences (Amendment) Act 2000 is, *"An Act to reduce the age at which, and to make provision with respect to the circumstances in which, certain sexual acts are lawful; to make it an offence for a person aged 18 or over to engage in sexual activity with or directed towards a person under that age if he is in a position of trust in relation to that person; and for connected purposes.* (This Act is also examined in the section of this booklet covering Protecting Children).

The Sexual Offences (Amendment) Act 2000 Act created a new offence to protect *"those under 18 years of age in particular areas from abuse of trust in the form of inappropriate sexual relationships"*. Although sexual relations with a child below the age of consent remains a criminal offence, the Home Office (in its 1999 booklet *"Caring for young people and the vulnerable? Guidance for preventing the abuse of trust"*) made it clear that the Bill (when enacted) would make unlawful *"any sexual intercourse (whether it is anal or vaginal) or other sexual activity between a person in a position of trust in certain defined areas and any person under 18 subject to their authority".* Furthermore, the Home Office guidance stated that neither *"homosexual or heterosexual relationships are acceptable within a position of trust; and they apply equally to all without regard to gender, race, religion, sexual orientation or disability".*

The Sexual Offences (Amendment) Act is, in fact, primarily concerned with ostensibly consensual behaviour within a relationship of trust. Thus, **a teacher (or any professional) in a position of trust with children aged 16 or 17 will now face conviction as a sex offender if he/she has sexual relations with a pupil - even if that pupil is aged 16 or 17 and has consented to the affair.** If a court finds a teacher guilty of this offence then he/she is highly likely to find himself/herself facing a custodial prison sentence. Furthermore, he/she will also be placed upon DfES List 99 and, consequently, be barred from teaching or working with children.

Although, the Home Office points out that "behaviour, such as cuddling another person when they are hurt or distressed or spontaneous activity such as celebratory embraces, for example on the sports field, would not normally be construed as sexual", it would be sensible and prudent for teachers to be very careful in any such situation. They should ensure that their actions – however innocent – cannot ever be misconstrued be a pupil or by others. As professional people, teachers should ensure that their behaviour is always of the highest standards. If a teacher ever finds himself or herself in a situation where an allegation of misconduct is made against them, they should, at once, ask their union for advice and assistance. Although the vast majority of all the misconduct allegations are subsequently found to be not proven, the best policy is for teachers to adhere always to practices that preclude any misconduct allegation ever being made.

Protecting Children

9. DfEE Circular 10/95 "Protecting Children from Abuse: the Role of the Education Service" and Appropriate Physical Contact with Pupils

DfEE Circular 10/95 explains how the education service can help to protect children from abuse. However, (although the Children Act 1989 has a much wider remit than this section), it must be pointed out that there is interrelationship and linkage with this booklet's section on the Children Act 1989. The main points of DfEE Circular 10/95 are that:

All staff should be alert to signs of abuse and know to whom they should report any concerns or suspicions.

All schools and colleges should have a designated member of staff responsible for co-ordinating action within the institution and liaising with other agencies, including the Area Child Protection Committee (ACPC).

All schools and colleges should be aware of the child protection procedures established by the ACPC and, where appropriate, by the local education authority.

All schools and colleges should have procedures (of which all staff should be aware) for handling suspected cases of abuse of pupils or students, including procedures if a member of staff is accused of abuse.

Staff with designated responsibility for child protection should receive appropriate training.

In every local education authority a senior officer should be responsible for co-ordinating action on child protection across the Authority.

For the purposes of the **child protection register** (a register of children at risk of abuse which is maintained by a local authority social services department or the National Society for the Prevention of Cruelty to Children [NSPCC] on behalf of a local social services department), DfEE Circular 10/95 defines four categories of abuse recognised for the child protection register. These are -

neglect: persistent or severe neglect, or the failure to protect a child from exposure to any kind of danger, including cold or starvation, or extreme failure to carry out important aspects of care, resulting in the significant impairment of the child's health or development, including non-organic failure to thrive;

physical injury: actual or likely physical injury to a child, or failure to prevent physical injury (or suffering) to a child including deliberate poisoning, suffocation and Munchausen's syndrome by proxy;

sexual abuse: actual or likely sexual exploitation of a child or adolescent; the child may be dependent and/or developmentally immature; and

emotional abuse: actual or likely severe adverse effect on the emotional and behavioural development of a child caused by persistent or severe emotional ill-treatment or rejection.

The DfEE Circular states "*An investigation into suspected abuse may result in a court making an emergency protection, care or supervision order if it is satisfied that a child is suffering, or is likely to suffer, 'significant harm'. 'Harm' means 'ill- treatment or the impairment of health or development'*" (Section 31 of the Children Act 1989).

DfEE Circular 10/95 points out the important fact that, "*because of their day to day contact with individual children, teachers and other staff in the education service are particularly well placed to observe outward signs of abuse, changes in behaviour or failure to develop*". These can take various physical forms such as bruises, lacerations and burns, or behavioural forms such as excessive dependence, attention seeking, precocity or withdrawal, etc. Teachers should be alert to any such signs, although the Circular makes it quite clear that these can do no more than give rise to suspicion.

In a school, a key element in ensuring that proper procedures are followed, is the **designated teacher**. The school's designated teacher (and all members of a school's staff should know who this person is), is the head teacher or another senior member of staff who is designated as having responsibility for liaising with the local authority social services department and the other agencies over signs of abuse. The DfEE Circular 10/95 states that designated teachers need to know:

how to identify the signs and symptoms of abuse and when to make a referral;

the local Area Child Protection Committee/Local Education Authority child protection procedures and the designated teacher's role within them;

the role and responsibilities of the investigating agencies and how to liaise with them;

the requirements of record-keeping; and

the conduct of a child protection conference and how the designated teacher or another member of staff can make an appropriate contribution to it.

The three principal agencies involved with child protection cases are the local authority social services department, the police, and the NSPCC. However, other agencies and support services can also be involved and these may include health professionals (including school nurses), education welfare services, education psychology services, probation services, etc. The designated teacher needs to establish a good working relationship with colleagues from the other agencies, especially the local social services department and the local police. As the DfEE Circular points out, this will "*help to build understanding, trust and confidence which will help to secure effective co-operation in cases of actual or suspected abuse*". (It is worth noting that OFSTED inspectors are required to assess a school's effectiveness in promoting the welfare, health, safety and guidance of its pupils and that, for part of the evidence for this judgement, they will look at the school's child protection policy and procedures).

If a child is placed on (or removed from) the local authority's child protection register (of children at risk) then the child's **key worker** from the local authority social services department should inform the school. Schools need to monitor these pupils in line with what has been agreed in the child protection plan. This might mean alerting the child's key worker or the Education Welfare Officer (EWO) if a child is absent or if signs suggest a deterioration in a pupil's home circumstances. Individual teachers clearly have an important monitoring role.

Schools and colleges should have procedures in place for handling cases of suspected abuse, including the procedures that must be followed if a teacher (or other member of staff) is accused of abuse. Designated teachers clearly have a very important role; not only should they know how to identify the signs and symptoms of abuse and when to make a referral, they must know when and how to liaise with the principal agencies and support services.

Although the Circular states that, *"Where teachers see any signs which cause them concern they should seek information from the child with tact and sympathy"*, if circumstances permit, it would be sensible to first seek advice from the designated teacher. Care must be taken in asking and interpreting a child's responses to questions about indications of possible abuse. **It is not the responsibility of teachers (or other school staff) to investigate suspected abuse, and they must not take action beyond that agreed in the procedures established by the local Area Child Protection Committee. If there are subsequent criminal proceedings, the way in which a teacher talks to a child could have an effect on the evidence which is put forward. Furthermore, no undertakings of absolute confidentiality should be given.** Leading questions should not be asked; rather things like "tell me what has happened" should be said. The child must be listened to very carefully and full notes taken (recording also the time, date and place and any other people present). The notes of the conversation should be passed to the designated teacher although the teacher who made the notes should be aware of the fact that the notes may need to be used in subsequent court proceedings.

Unfortunately there are occasions when pupils (or their parents) accuse teachers (or other members of staff) of physically or sexually abusing them. Although, in many cases, such allegations are false, regrettably some are true. If an allegation of abuse is made then it is most important that the matter is dealt with properly, and that it follows the agreed school policy. This is a very serious matter and, even if the allegation is false, can result in long term damage to the health and career of a teacher. The teacher unions and the Council of Local Education Authorities have produced guidance procedures (endorsed by the Association of Directors of Social Services and the Association of Chief Police Officers), in line with Area Child Protection Committee practice and not compromising child protection, yet designed to minimise the very damaging effects of false allegations. Schools (and individual teachers) should all consider ways to reduce the risk of allegations being made.

The DfEE Circular does point out that *"it is unnecessary and unrealistic to suggest that teachers should touch pupils only in emergencies. Particularly with younger pupils, touching them is inevitable and can give welcome reassurance to the child. However, teachers must bear in mind that even perfectly innocent actions can be misconstrued".* Teachers, therefore, should act appropriately and not *"touch pupils, however casually, in ways or on parts of the body that might be considered indecent".*

However, it is a fact of life in schools that, on occasions, teachers and pupils make physical contact. This is especially true in primary schools where, for example, teachers sometimes help pupils to tie shoelaces or ties, comfort children in distress, and help when (as occasionally happens) a child has become soiled. In secondary schools, although there is much reduced physical contact (because the children are older), there may be occasions when this occurs; for example, a physical education teacher in the school gymnasium often needs to support/catch a child when they are landing after vaulting. However, teachers should be aware that some children might, for a variety of reasons, find being touched by a teacher either uncomfortable or even distressing. Therefore, a teacher needs to be sensitive to a child's reactions and always to act appropriately as the circumstances dictate.

Furthermore, in extreme (but fortunately rare) cases a teacher may physically have to restrain a pupil to prevent him or her causing injury to himself or herself, or to others, or to property. In any such cases, the DfEE's advice to teachers is to use no more than the **minimum force** necessary and to avoid causing any injury to the pupil. This aspect is dealt with more fully in the next chapter of this document.

Every teacher should bear in mind the very important point that even perfectly innocent actions can sometimes be misconstrued by children or their parents (and that this has sometimes been done mischievously). As well as always acting professionally and appropriately, teachers also need to think about and be aware of potential dangers. To minimise the risk of allegations of teacher misconduct, it is suggested that schools, in consultation with the local authority and Area Child Protection Committee, draw up and implement a "Code of Conduct" and, to avoid any misunderstandings, ensure parents are aware of the agreed code and what it contains. On being appointed to a school, teachers should ask if such a code exists; if it does, then they should read it very carefully and ensure that they always act upon it.

As professional people, teachers must ensure that their behaviour is always of the highest standards. Both employers and senior staff have a responsibility to ensure: (a) that professional behaviour applies at all times to relationships between staff and students; (b) that all staff are clear about what constitutes appropriate behaviour and professional boundaries; (c) that those boundaries are maintained, with the sensitive support and supervision that may be required. This is obviously particularly important in circumstances where there is one to one contact with pupils (such as in an individual music lesson) and in residential schools or residential situations such as field trips.

If a teacher is ever in a situation where an allegation of misconduct is made, he/she should at once ask his/her union for advice and assistance.

It used to be possible for someone barred from direct employment as a teacher to circumvent a ban by working either as a volunteer in a school or college or in a business contracted to provide services to a school or college (examples being catering, maintenance or transport). To protect children from all such individuals, the Criminal Records Bureau Enhanced Disclosure check now extends to volunteers, school governors, and staff employed by contractors who will have regular contact with children and young people attending the school or college either on or off the premises. Volunteers to whom this applies are people who regularly help in classrooms; in extracurricular activities such as study support or sports coaching; or in supervising pupils on holidays organised by or for the school or college.

10. DfEE Circular 11/95 "Misconduct of Teachers and Workers with Children and Young Persons"

The first thing to note is that although the DfEE Circular 11/95 is listed under Protecting Children in the 2002 DfES/TTA Guidance on the Standards for the Award of Qualified Teacher Status, the Circular has been discontinued by the DfES. However, because the Circular's principal objectives still hold true, and because it contained useful information, the key features of DfEE Circular 11/95 are described in this booklet. It should be noted that DfEE Circular 11/95 was written well before the formation of the General Teaching Council and its *"Code of Professional Values and Practice"* was published, and before the Criminal Records Bureau and the statutory requirement for teachers to undergo the Enhanced Disclosure procedure came into existence. (It will also be noted that there is some overlap in this section with what is written in the Employment section of this booklet.)

DfEE Circular 11/95 described in detail the powers of the Secretary of State to bar someone from employment as a teacher (or other post working with children or other young persons) on grounds of misconduct, and also gave guidance to employers and teacher training institutions about reporting cases of misconduct by teachers or students.

DfEE Circular number 11/95 listed seven sexual offences where, if a person was found guilty of a sexual offence which involved a child under the age of sixteen, would lead to automatic barring from employment as a teacher. The seven sexual offences were: rape, buggery, incest, unlawful sexual intercourse, indecent assault, gross indecency, and taking or distributing indecent photographs (the latter offence would, of course, include Internet misuse – see next paragraph). The Circular also identified nine other varieties of behaviour likely to lead to barring. These were: violent behaviour towards children or young people; a sexual, or otherwise inappropriate, relationship with a pupil, regardless of whether the pupil is over the legal age of consent (and, it should be noted, that DfEE Circular 11/95 was written before the Sexual Offences (Amendment) Act 2000 was passed); a sexual offence against someone over the age of sixteen; any offence involving serious violence; drug trafficking and other drug related offences; stealing school property or monies; deception in relation to employment as a teacher or at a school, for example false claims about qualifications, or failure to disclose past convictions; any conviction which results in a sentence of more than 12 months imprisonment; and repeated misconduct or multiple convictions unless of a very minor nature.

In 2002 the media reported reported on two teachers (one a head teacher) who had been found to have pornographic pictures of children on their personal computers. It is a criminal offence in Britain, punishable by up to ten years in prison, to make or possess indecent photographs of children. People who knowingly receive pictures of child pornography on their personal computers by e-mail are guilty of the offence of possession. Anyone who deliberately downloads any such pictures from the internet is deemed guilty of the offence of making a photograph. Furthermore, the same applies to those who knowingly send child pornography to others.

The Circular discussed the kind of behaviour which was regarded as misconduct requiring consideration by the Secretary of State. This was: (a) committing a criminal offence resulting in a conviction; (b) behaviour which could lead to prosecution for a criminal offence; and (c) behaviour which involved an abuse of a teacher's position of trust or a breach of the standards of propriety expected of the profession. (However, DfEE Circular 11/95 stated that convictions for minor traffic offences, and some lesser offences, were not normally regarded as misconduct and, furthermore, neither should a teacher's private sexual activities unless the latter involved the kind of behaviour referred to in a, b or c above).

In DfEE Circular 11/95, the purpose of barring people from employment on grounds of misconduct as a teacher or worker with children or young persons was stated clearly:

"The Secretary of State's principal concerns are:
- to safeguard children and young people from contact with people who are deemed unsuitable, either because the person presents a risk to their safety or welfare, or because the person's behaviour presents an unacceptable example to them
- to uphold the high standards of behaviour expected of members of the teaching profession, and

- to protect schools and the education service generally from fraud or deception."

Today, as in 1995, if a person is barred from teaching or working with children or young persons, then their name, date of birth and teacher reference number is entered on DfES List 99. Furthermore, he/she would also be "struck off" the Register of Teachers which is maintained by the General Teaching Council.

Some of the procedures contained and suggested within DfEE Circular 11/95 have been superseded because of: (a) the formation of the General Teaching Council; and (b) the statutory requirement for teachers to undergo the Criminal Records Bureau's Enhanced Disclosure check. Furthermore, the passing of the Sexual Offences (Amendment) Act 2000 means the list of sexual offences contained in the Circular requires some amendment. Nevertheless, the general purpose, provisions and guidance of DfEE Circular 11/95 stand the test of time and few in the teaching profession would disagree with the Circular's key objective: "*to safeguard children and young people from contact with people who are deemed unsuitable, either because the person presents a risk to their safety or welfare, or because the person's behaviour presents an unacceptable example to them*".

11. The Children Act 1989, especially Section 3(5) on what is reasonable in safeguarding and promoting children's welfare

The Children Act 1989 reformed the law relating to children and it replaced much previous legislation. The Act aims to provide for local authority services for children in need and others; to amend the law with respect to children's homes, community homes, voluntary homes and voluntary organisations; to make provision with respect to fostering, child minding and day care for young children and adoption; and for connected purposes. In the Children Act 1989 a "child" means a person under the age of eighteen.

The basic feature underpinning the Children Act 1989 is the legal obligation **to ensure the welfare of children who may be at risk**. Under the Act, local authorities have a statutory duty to identify the extent to which there are children at risk or in need within their area. Through the provision of services, local authorities must take reasonable steps to prevent children suffering neglect or ill treatment.

The Children Act 1989 has real teeth. In a child's interests, a local authority is empowered to take a variety of actions in the courts (normally the magistrates' family proceedings court) to ensure the welfare of a child. In the child's interests, a court can make various court orders; four of these (contact orders, prohibited steps orders, residence orders and specific issue orders) are detailed in Section 8 (1) of the Children Act and, consequently, are known as "Section 8 orders". These are defined:

> "a contact order" means an order requiring the person with whom a child lives, or is to live, to allow the child to visit or stay with the person named in the order, or for that person and the child otherwise to have contact with each other;

> "a prohibited steps order" means an order that no step which could be taken by a parent in meeting his parental responsibility

for a child, and which is of a kind specified in the order, shall be taken by any person without the consent of the court;

"a residence order" means an order settling the arrangements to be made as to the person with whom a child is to live; and

"a specific issue order" means an order giving directions for the purpose of determining a specific question which has arisen, or which may arise, in connection with any aspect of parental responsibility for a child.

Furthermore, an *"education supervision order"* (which is defined in Section 36 of the Act) is another order which a court can make *if it is satisfied that a child is of compulsory school age and is not being properly educated.* When an education supervision order is made, a supervisor is appointed. Schedule 3, Part III, Section 12 of the Act defines the effect of education supervision orders:

Where an education supervision order is in force with respect to a child, it shall be the duty of the supervisor -
(a)　to advise, to assist and befriend, and give directions to -
(i) the supervised child; and
(ii) his parents,
(b)　in such a way as will, in the opinion of the supervisor, secure that he is properly educated.

Furthermore, before the supervisor gives any directions under these regulations:

The supervisor shall, so far as is reasonably practicable, ascertain the wishes and feelings of -
(a)　the child; and
(b)　his parents,
including, in particular, their wishes as to the place at which the child should be educated.

Section 3 of the Children Act defines "parental responsibility" as *all the rights, duties, powers, responsibilities and authority which by law a parent of a child has in relation to the child and his property.* However, Section 3, paragraph 5 states –

(5)　A person who -
(a) does not have parental responsibility for a particular child; but

(b) has care of the child,

may (subject to the provisions of this Act) do what is reasonable in all the circumstances of the case for the purpose of safeguarding or promoting the child's welfare.

It is clear, therefore, that Section 3 (5) of the Children Act applies to teachers in their relations with pupils. Furthermore, the important fact that the Children Act gives statutory backing to the teacher, should the teacher need to provide emergency help or care to a child (such as a child in a dangerous situation on a field trip), should be noted.

Because teachers are often in positions to discover, notice or suspect that a child is being ill-treated, it is very important that teachers play their part in the process of identifying any children who may be at risk. If a teacher discovers, notices or suspects that a child is being, or has been, ill-treated or abused, then they should discuss it immediately with the school's **designated teacher**. This person (normally the head or a senior teacher) is responsible for liaising on child abuse issues with the local designated agencies. In such circumstances, the designated teacher normally liaises with the local agencies and support services and contributes relevant information; if deemed necessary, a court can be asked to make an emergency protection, care or supervision order (see also the Protecting Children section in this booklet on DfEE Circular 10/95).

The local authority, or a primary feeder school (in the case of a secondary school), may inform the school that a particular child is on the child protection register and/or that a court order is in force. In such cases, teachers should all do their best to keep a watching eye on the child; however, this is often easier said than done. If, for example, a court order forbids contact with a particular parent, then it is extremely difficult for the school to know if that particular parent is waiting, with other parents, for the child outside the school gates.

When in charge of pupils, teachers are *"in loco parentis"* (in the place of parents), with all the responsibility that this entails. **When children are at school, or engaged in educational activities off the school site, Section 3(5) of the Children Act requires that teachers must do what is reasonable in all the circumstances of the case for the purpose of safeguarding or promoting the child's welfare.** Because teachers must, to a greater or lesser extent, take the place of the parents when children are in their charge, they should always act as though they (the teachers) had the parental responsibility for the pupils in their care.

12. The Sexual Offences (Amendment) Act 2000, Section 3, and the Home Office 1999 publication "Caring for young people and the vulnerable? Guidance for preventing abuse of trust"

In this booklet, the section on employment contains advice on the employment aspects of the Sexual Offences (Amendment) Act 2000. There is, therefore, a certain amount of replication. Because the Home Office 1999 publication *"Caring for young people and the vulnerable? Guidance for preventing abuse of trust"* is closely related to what the Sexual Offences (Amendment) Act 2000 contains, these two documents are dealt with together in this chapter.

In England, Wales and Scotland, the age of consent for heterosexual sex is 16 (Northern Ireland is 17) and, therefore, young people of 16 and over (or 17 and over in Northern Ireland) can legally consent to some types of sexual activity. However, the Sexual Offences (Amendment) Act 2000 created a new offence to protect *"those under 18 years of age in particular areas from abuse of trust in the form of inappropriate sexual relationships"*. As far as full-time education is concerned, the Act has made consensual sexual relationships illegal between a member of staff in a position of trust and pupils over the legal age of consent but under the age of eighteen. The Act states its purpose: *"An Act to reduce the age at which, and to make provision with respect to the circumstances in which, certain sexual acts are lawful; to make it an offence for a person aged 18 or over to engage in sexual activity with or directed towards a person under that age if he is in a position of trust in relation to that person; and for connected purposes.*

The Sexual Offences (Amendment) Act 2000 states that, for the purposes of Section 3 of the Act, a person aged 18 or over ("A") is in a position of trust in relation to a person under that age ("B") if any of several conditions are fulfilled. Condition 4 relates specifically to educational institutions (be they schools, colleges or universities) and the Act states, *"The fourth condition is that A looks after persons under 18 who are receiving full-time education at an educational institution, and B is receiving edu-*

cation at that institution." The Act states what is meant by a person in a position of trust as, "*A person looks after persons under 18 … if he is regularly involved in caring for, training, supervising or being in sole charge of such persons*" and this, clearly, covers teachers and lecturers. For the purpose of the Act, a person who receives full-time education is defined as, "*a person receives full-time education at an educational institution if – (a) he is registered or otherwise enrolled as a full-time pupil or student at the institution; or (b) he receives education at the institution under arrangements with another educational institution at which he is so registered or otherwise enrolled*".

Section 3 of the Sexual Offences (Amendment) Act 2000 defines what is meant by the abuse of a position of trust:

3. – (1) Subject to subsections (2) and (3) below, it shall be an offence for a person aged 18 or over-

(a) to have sexual intercourse (whether vaginal or anal) with a person under that age; or

(b) to engage in any other sexual activity with or directed towards such a person,

if (in either case) he is in a position of trust in relation to that person.

(2) Where a person ("A") is charged with an offence under this section of having sexual intercourse with, or engaging in any sexual activity with or directed towards, another person ("B"), it shall be a defence for A to prove that, at the time of the intercourse or activity –

(a) he did not know, and could not reasonably have been expected to know, that B was under 18;

(b) he did not know, and could not reasonably have been expected to know, that B was a person in relation to whom he was in a position of trust; or

(c) he was lawfully married to B.

(3) It shall not be an offence under this section for a person ("A") to have sexual intercourse with, or engage in any other sexual activity with or directed towards, another person ("B") if immediately before the commencement of this Act –

(a) A was in a position of trust in relation to B; and

(b) a sexual relationship existed between them.

(4) A person guilty of an offence under this section shall be liable –

(a) on summary conviction (a "summary offence" is one which is tried by a magistrate), to imprisonment for a term not exceeding six months, or to a fine no exceeding the statutory maximum, or to both;

(b) on conviction on indictment (an "indictment" is the formal written accusation of someone who is tried by jury), to imprisonment for a term not exceeding five years, or to a fine, or to both.

(5) In this section, "sexual" activity" –

(a) does not include any activity which a reasonable person would regard as sexual only with knowledge of the intentions, motives or feelings of the parties; but

(b) subject to that, means any activity which such as person would regard as sexual in all the circumstances.

Pre-existing legislation (the Sexual Offences Act 1956, Indecency with Children Act 1960, Criminal Law Act 1977 and Protection of Children Act 1978) protects children below 16 years of age and, thus, the new legislation introduced in the Sexual Offences (Amendment) Act 2000 is, in reality, only likely to affect those teaching pupils aged 16 and 17. The important fact that all those teaching pupils aged 16 and 17 should always be aware of is that if a teacher in a position of trust has sexual relations with a pupil aged 16 or 17 – then even if the pupil has consented to the affair - he/she faces conviction as a sex offender. If a court finds the teacher guilty of the offence then he/she is likely to find himself/herself facing a custodial prison sentence. Furthermore, they will have the conviction entered against their name on the Police National Computer with a special mark to indicate that they have been found guilty of a sexual offence. They will also be placed upon DfES List 99 and, consequently, be barred from teaching or working with children.

In 1999, the Home Office issued guidance information in its booklet, *"Caring for young people and the vulnerable? Guidance for preventing the abuse of trust".* Although the Home Office booklet pre-dates the Sexual Offences (Amendment) Act 2000, it needs to be read alongside the Act because the guidance was written whilst the Sexual Offences (Amendment) Bill was proceeding through parliament and the information in the booklet relates directly to the Act.

The 1999 Home Office booklet is explicit and it defines what the government means by sexual activity: *"activity which would normally be recognised as sexual … obvious examples include sexual intercourse, oral sex and masturbation"*. The Home Office guidance states that neither *"homosexual or heterosexual relationships are acceptable within a position of trust; and they apply equally to all without regard to gender, race, religion, sexual orientation or disability"*. The Home Office strongly recommends that all organisations which work with young people or vulnerable adults - and this includes schools - should produce their own policies (in the light of the principles laid down in the guidance booklet) to suit their own individual circumstances, for the protection of those in their care from sexual and other forms of abuse.

Finally, although, the Home Office points out that *"behaviour, such as cuddling another person when they are hurt or distressed or spontaneous activity such as celebratory embraces, for example on the sports field, would not normally be construed as sexual"*, it would be sensible and prudent for teachers to be very careful in all such situations. Teachers should always ensure that their actions – however innocent – cannot ever be misconstrued be a pupil or by others. As professional people, teachers should ensure that their behaviour is always of the highest standards.

13. Teachers' Common Law Duty To Ensure That Pupils Are Healthy And Safe On School Premises And When Leading Activities Off The School Site, Such As Educational Visits, School Outings Or Field Trips

In the first and second editions of this booklet, written to meet what was contained in Section D ("Other Professional Requirements") of Annex A of DfEE Circular 4/98, there was a section devoted to teachers' common law duty of care for their pupils. Although the 2002 Guidance on the Standards for the Award of Qualified Teacher Status does not list this subject, the author nevertheless believes this is an import omission. In the last few years, several pupils have died whilst on educational visits and, therefore, under the section Protecting Children, the author feels it is most important that all teachers have an understanding of this particular subject.

Furthermore, it also needs to be pointed out that there is considerable overlap and interrelationship between teachers' common law duty of care (to ensure that the pupils they are responsible for are healthy and safe) and the Health and Safety at Work Act 1974.

Legal systems exist to do justice between (a) individuals and (b) individuals and the state. English common law has been evolving for over a thousand years and it could be described as both (a) the law of the common people and (b) the law of the judges (where the judges represent the interests of the ordinary person). English common law is the traditional law that remains today in the areas where Acts of Parliament (which are statutory law) have not intervened. The doctrine of "precedent" underpins English common law. In the doctrine of precedent, common law courts (with certain technical but important exceptions) are legally bound to follow the earlier decisions (known as "precedents") of previous courts (the earlier decisions being reported in the law reports). As far as the common law duty of care is concerned, the case law really started to appear in the nineteenth century, when early casualties of the industrial revolution began to sue in the courts for compensation for injuries they received whilst at work.

All employees are bound by the duty of obligation of care imposed by the area of common law concerned with the **tort of negligence**. A tort (French for fault) is a civil wrong and is a breach of a general duty that is imposed by the law. It is remediable by a civil action in the courts for "unliquidated damages" (where the amount of the damages is left to the discretion of the court).

As a tort, negligence involves three elements. These are:

(a)   a legal duty of care owed by one person to another;
(b)   a breach of this duty by the person owing the duty of care; and
(c)   damage to the person, to whom the duty of care is owed, which is caused as a result of the breach of duty of care.

The consequences of an employee not taking reasonable care, or acting carelessly, are that:

(a)   a co-employee or a third party (this could be a member of the (b) public or, in the case of a school, a pupil) may be injured or killed or
(b)   the employee may be injured or killed.

In law, we all owe a duty of care to our neighbour, our neighbour being defined as anyone who we can reasonably foresee would be likely to be injured by our acts or omissions; for teachers, our neighbour includes the pupils in their care. Furthermore, in Winfield (1989) the concept of reasonableness and professionals is stated, *"Where anyone practises a profession, the law expects him to show the amount of competence associated with the proper discharge of the duties of that profession"*. This clearly indicates that teachers must always consider carefully the safety of their pupils. A teacher's actions must ensure that whenever they are in charge of pupils, whether on or off the school site, the pupils' safety is never compromised.

In the eyes of the law, **children are not considered to think in the same way as adults** (children being defined in Health and Safety legislation as persons under compulsory school-leaving age, i.e. under sixteen). Adults should be able to see potential danger areas that a child may not be able to recognise. Therefore teachers have to think on behalf of their pupils and, if a teacher sees a pupil(s) doing something dangerous or potentially dangerous, then it is their legal duty to try to stop that action so that the safety of the pupil(s) is not compromised. It should be noted that almost all "accidents" are preventable.

In every school there are areas of potential danger (such as corridors, stairs, offices, classrooms, laboratories, canteens, halls/gymnasiums, playgrounds and sports fields). Teachers need to be aware of all potential danger areas - and where particular behaviour or actions of pupils (or adults) could compromise safety. Furthermore, for school activities like chemistry lessons, physical education and games, etc. an even greater standard of care is required. If would also be wise, as the case of *Affutu –v- Clarke (1984)* demonstrates, that teachers should not take part in games with children. In this case, a teacher injured a pupil after high tackling a boy in possession of the ball. The court held that the teacher was negligent because he had not taken account of his skill, experience and physical advantages.

The landmark case of *Fitzgerald -v- Northcote (1865)* established that, while a pupil is under a teacher's control, the authority and responsibility of a teacher in relation to a pupil is broadly the same as a parent in relation to a child. Often referred to as *"in loco parentis"*, it means that on sending a child to school, parents delegate their own authority to the teacher so far as is necessary for the child's welfare and so far as is reasonable to maintain discipline both in the interests of the individual pupil and of the school. A teacher who takes a party of children away from school remains *in loco parentis* throughout the trip and the responsibility cannot be delegated to anyone else. The courts expect teachers to take appropriate care having regard to the nature of the visit. The more hazardous or demanding the trip, the younger or less able the pupils, then the greater will be the level of care that is required.

If teachers take pupils off the school premises on an educational visit, school outing or field trip, then (as described in this booklet's Employment section on the Health and Safety at Work Act 1974), it is important that a **risk assessment** is formally undertaken before the activity commences. Once off the school site, a completely new set of potential dangers, such as traffic dangers, must be considered and planned for. It would be very wise to read and comply with the practice suggested in the DfES's good practice guide *"Health and Safety of Pupils on Educational Visits (2001)*.

There are potential dangers associated with certain activities and locations and, tragically, pupils have sometimes died whilst off the school site. Several times, as a member of a mountain rescue team, the author of this document helped to search for and recover the bodies of children (taking part in off school site activities and supervised by teachers) who had died on mountains and in rivers. The Lyme Bay canoeing tragedy of a few years ago was a similar circumstance and, in this particular landmark case, legal action for breach of the duty of care took place. Although the legal principle of vicarious liability was utilised (see the introduction to this booklet), both employer and employees were cross-examined in court.

It is well worth noting that, although accidents do occur in the school and its immediate surroundings, most of the accidents that the legal departments of the teaching unions have to deal with occur when pupils are engaged in activities (such as field trips and educational visits) off the school site. The death of (or a serious accident to) a pupil in a teacher's care - particularly if there is any question of negligence - is a very serious matter indeed. In such circumstances the teacher should immediately contact the legal department of his/her union for professional advice.

In 1865, Edward Whymper and his party of seven reached the summit of the Matterhorn. After this successful first ascent of the mountain, four of his party fell to their deaths on the descent. To conclude this section it is very well worth considering Whymper's words when he wrote about the tragedy in 1871. *"Courage and strength are nought without prudence, and that a momentary negligence may destroy the happiness of a lifetime. Do nothing in haste; look well to each step; and from the beginning, think what may be the end."* These are wise words and teachers would be well advised to heed them.

14. The Health and Safety at Work Act 1974

The Employment section in this booklet shows how the Health and Safety at Work Act 1974 affects teachers as employees. **Teachers, however, also have a responsibility under the Act for the health and safety of their pupils.** Although not listed in the Protecting Children section of the 2002 Guidance to the Standards for the Award of Qualified Teacher Status, it is important that teachers observe their statutory responsibilities for their pupils under the Act. The Act helps protect children whilst at school (and on educational visits, etc.) which is why it is also covered in the Protecting Children section of this booklet. There is some, however, some necessary repetition. It is also important to note that teachers' responsibilities under the Health and Safety at Work Act 1974 are closely interrelated with their common law duty of care for their pupils (see the preceding chapter of this booklet).

Although much of the Health and Safety at Work Act legislation is aimed at workplaces with obvious dangers (such as farms, quarries and factories), schools possess potential danger areas (such as corridors, stairs, offices, classrooms, laboratories, canteens, halls/gymnasiums, playgrounds and sports fields) and schools must comply fully with the Act's provisions. It is worth noting that 1 in 12 of the accidents reported to the Health and Safety Executive occur in education establishments.

Much of the Health and Safety at Work Act is concerned with the duties of employers, and their responsibility for their employees. However, both Section 7 and Section 8 of the Act makes it clear that every employee in an organisation also has personal responsibilities.

The general statutory duties of employees are stated in the Act:

7.   It shall be the duty of every employee while at work –
      (a) to take reasonable care for the health and safety of him-

self and of other persons who may be affected by his acts or
omissions at work; and

(b)   as regards any duty or requirement imposed on his employer,
or any other person by or under any of the relevant statutory
provisions, to co-operate with him so far as is necessary to
enable that duty to be performed or complied with.

It should be noted that, as far as schools are concerned, in (a) "other persons" includes pupils and members of the public (such as parents) and in (b) "any other person" could be the head teacher or the head of a department, etc.

Under the Health and Safety at Work Act 1974, all lawful visitors to premises are entitled to protection. In the case of schools, parents and other visiting adults clearly all fall within this provision. However, the position of pupils under the Act is not altogether apparent because they are not visitors or employees. However, Section 2(3)(a) of the Occupiers' Liability Act 1957 states that occupiers "*must be prepared for children to be less careful than adults*". Therefore, it is clear that both the school and individual teachers each have responsibilities for the health, safety and welfare of pupils whilst the pupils are in their care.

Because Section 7 of the Health and Safety at Work Act 1974 places a personal responsibility for ensuring health and safety at work, teachers have a statutory duty to report anything they believe is dangerous (e.g. a hole in the school playground, dangerous chairs in a classroom, etc.) and (for protection) this is best done in writing and a copy kept. Once the employee has formally reported the perceived danger they are absolved of responsibility and the employer has to consider the matter. If the employer does nothing then, should there be an accident, the employer might be found to be negligent. However, if an employee notices something they believe is dangerous and does not report it then, should an accident occur, the employee could be guilty of contributory negligence

Section 8 of the Act states that employees have a duty not to interfere with or misuse anything that an employer has provided for safety purposes according to statutory requirements.

8.   No person shall intentionally or recklessly interfere with or
misuse anything provided in the interests of health, safety
or welfare in pursuance of any of the relevant statutory
provisions.

For example, when schools provide safety clothing (such as safety goggles for use in science lessons) or safety equipment (such as fire extinguishers), then they must not be misused and they must always be left in the correct locations. Clearly teachers have individual responsibility for ensuring that this practice is adhered to. For example, if a teacher sees safety clothing or safety equipment being misused (fire extinguishers are sometimes misused by pupils), then the individual teacher has a duty to report that the occurrence.

As far as health and safety at work is concerned, there is an implied condition that employees will carry out their duties with reasonable skill and not to be negligent. As far as teachers are concerned, this implied condition has major implications. There is a clear duty for teachers to carry out all their duties professionally and to take very great care to avoid getting into a situation where the safety of a pupil(s) could be in danger through any **negligence** on the teacher's part. If it is shown that a pupil(s) (or others) have come to harm because of a teacher's negligence, then the consequences for the teacher could be disastrous.

For a teacher to be legally liable for damages in the case of an accident the law requires the injured party (in the case of a pupil this would usually be the child's parents) must show that, on balance of probability, the teacher was negligent. Under English law there does not have to be any *intention* to hurt anyone. The question the court will ask is, "would a reasonable person have acted in the same way in similar circumstances?"

Pupils (and sometimes teachers) do sustain injuries whilst they are at school. Schools (as employers) are required to keep Accident Books and must report certain injuries (such as some types of fracture and eye injuries) to the Health and Safety Executive under The Reporting of Injuries, Diseases and Dangerous Occurrences Regulations 1985. If an accident occurs (to pupils or staff) it is important to ensure that a formal entry is made in the Accident Book, and this includes accidents that happen off the school premises. (Most schools have a set procedure for this.) Unless this is done, it could be difficult, at a later date, to prove how/when an accident took place. It is also important to consider the accident objectively to see if similar accidents could be prevented in the future.

Much of the recent health and safety at work legislation has been concerned with the assessment of risk. Employees (as well as employers) have risk assessment responsibilities; this is something that involves individual teachers. For example, if a teacher wishes to take a class off the school premises for a geography field trip, the teacher, when planning the field trip, must carry out a thorough assessment of any potential risks to both pupils and accompanying adults. Unless this is done properly, and it can be shown that this was done properly, then both the teacher and their employer could find themselves in difficulty defending a charge of negligence if an accident occurs.

One important area of health and safety legislation which affects schools is fire precautions. The health and safety of all the occupants (employees, visitors and pupils), in particular their safe escape in the event of fire, must be reasonably assured. Fire practices, therefore, should be carried out regularly and all teachers should know the school's safety and emergency procedures.

A final word is necessary regarding pupils and medication. The administration of medication to pupils is not within the teachers' contract of employment and, normally, it is a pupil's parents who are responsible for their child's medication. There are very real dangers in a teacher deciding to give medication that has not been prescribed by a medical practitioner to a child. Teachers are not qualified medical practitioners and they do not know the full medical background of the child (such as the possibility of the child having an allergic reaction to a particular drug). Furthermore, teachers must not take the decision to administer even prescribed medication to a pupil(s), or give a pupil(s) permission to take medicine unless they are in situations such as an educational visit. In such a situation, the pupil's parents must (before the visit) provide the school with written details of what medication is required, the dosage, times of dosage, and their written consent for a teacher (or the pupil) to administer the medication. Local education authorities have very strict policies concerning the giving of medication and there is general information regarding medication, together with specific guidance on the control of asthma, epilepsy, diabetes and anaphylaxis, in the good practice guide accompanying Circular 14/96 *"Supporting Pupils with Medical Needs in School"*. (See also the section concerning DfEE Circular 14/96 in the Special Educational Needs/Disability section of this booklet).

15. Appropriate Physical Restraint of Pupils (Section 4 of the Education Act 1997, DfE Circular 9/94 and DH LAC (94) 9 "The Education of Children with Emotional and Behavioural Difficulties" and DfEE Circular 10/98 "Section 550A of the Education Act 1996: The Use of Force to Control or Restrain Pupils")

Although this subject and these two documents do not appear on the DfES/TTA list of documents in the Protecting Children section of the 2002 *Guidance to the Standards for the Award of Qualified Teacher Status,* this particular subject is, nevertheless, very important in the context of Protecting Children and it has, therefore, been included in the Protecting Children section of this booklet.

Paragraph 115 of DfE Circular 9/94 (*"The Education of Children with Emotional and Behavioural Difficulties"*) contains guidance on when, and how, teachers should restrain pupils physically. The Circular states that, *"On rare occasions there is no alternative to restraining pupils physically, in their and others' interests and safety,"* but that *"no more than the minimum necessary force should be used"* and *"such interventions should be made only when they are likely to succeed".* Because, there is obviously potential for a subsequent charge of assault, it is wise to act with the utmost prudence in any such situation and *"desirably, more than one adult should be present".* Furthermore, the DfE Circular makes it quite clear that teachers *"are not expected to restrain a child if by doing so they will put themselves at risk".*

The DfE Circular states that *"physical restraint is normally necessary only to prevent a pupil causing harm to him or herself or to others, seriously damaging property, or committing some criminal act which risks harm to people or property, when verbal commands will not control the behaviour".* The purpose of intervention is *"to restore safety, and restraint should not continue for longer than is necessary".* The DfE Circular states very clearly that *"physical contact and restraint should never be used in anger and teachers must seek to avoid any injury to the child".*

If faced with this sort of situation, a teacher should always consider whether there is any alternative to physical restraint. For example (as the DfE Circular points out), it is sometimes more effective to persuade an agitated child to move to a calmer environment than holding them or physically restraining them. Deflection can be more effective than confrontation.

Although largely applicable to young people living in children's homes, rather than for schools, the Department of Health guidance *"Permissible Forms of Control in Children's Residential Care" (1993)*, offers positive, practical advice on the care and control of young people which teachers may find useful. This document contains advice such as when it is appropriate to use physical restraint and more moderate methods of control.

Compared with teachers who work in mainstream schools, those who teach in special schools are probably more likely to experience pupils who may require complex or repeated physical management. All such children should have a prescribed, written handling policy; their parents should be informed how restraint will be exercised; and, staff who have to deal with these pupils should be trained in proper and safe methods of restraint.

Three years after DfE Circular 9/94 was published, the Education Act 1997 became law. As well as amending earlier education legislation, the Act gave statutory force of law to the teachers' power to restrain pupils. Section 4 of the Education Act 1997 states:

(1)   A member of the staff of the school may use, in relation to any pupil at the school, such force as is reasonable in the circumstances for the purpose of preventing the pupil from doing (or continuing to do) any of the following, namely –
(a) committing any offence,
(b) causing personal injury to, or damage to the property of, any person (including the pupil himself), or
(c) engaging in any behaviour prejudicial to the maintenance of good order and discipline at the school or among any of its pupils, whether that behaviour occurs during a teaching lesson or otherwise.

(2)   Subsection (1) [i.e. paragraph 1 above] applies where a member of the staff of a school is –
(a) on the premises of the school, or
(b) elsewhere at a time when, as a member of its staff, he has lawful control or charge of the pupil concerned;
but it does not authorise anything to be done in relation to a pupil which constitutes the giving of corporal punishment

within the meaning of section 548 [of the Education Act 1996, which states there is no right to give corporal punishment].

(3)   Subsection (1) [i.e. paragraph 1 above] shall not be taken to prevent any person from relying on any defence available to him otherwise than by virtue of this section.

(4)   In this section -
"member of staff", in relation to a school, means any teacher who works at the school and any other person who, with the authority of the head teacher, has lawful control or charge of pupils at the school;
"offence" includes anything that would be an offence but for the operation of any presumption that a person under a particular age is incapable of committing an offence.

Under the Education Act 1997, therefore, a teacher is permitted by law to use reasonable force to prevent pupils committing offences; causing personal injury to, or damage to the property of another person (including the pupil); and engaging in forms of behaviour that are prejudicial to the maintenance of good order and discipline at the school. Teachers are also permitted to take restraining action both on the school premises and when they have lawful control (such as on a field trip). However, it is instructive to remember the extremely distressing experiences that Marjorie Evans, the head teacher of a large junior school in Monmouthshire, went through in 2000 after restraining an unruly pupil. The pupil (falsely) alleged that Marjorie Evans had slapped him across the face. Eventually, after a lengthy suspension from duties and highly distressing experiences and appearances in the courts, Marjorie Evans was found to be completely innocent of all charges and she was reinstated in post. However, this demonstrates just how careful teachers now have to be when using physical force to control or restrain pupils. **Teachers should always be mindful of the possibility of a subsequent claim of assault and so they should act with utmost prudence and use only the minimum necessary force.**

By adding Section 550A to the Education Act 1996, the Education Act 1997 clarified the position concerning the use of physical force by teachers to control or restrain pupils. This came into force on 1 September 1998 and applies to all schools. The definitive guidance document is now DfEE Circular 10/98 *"Section 550A of the Education Act: The Use of Force to Control or Retrain Pupils"* and all teachers and schools must follow these guidelines.

DfEE Circular 10/98 points out that, since the Children Act 1989, there has been a common misconception that any physical contact with a child is unlawful but that belief is not correct. Where necessary, reasonable force can be used to control or to restrain pupils. However, Circular 10/98 makes it clear there is no legal definition of "reasonable force" and that it will always depend on all the circumstances of the particular case. The use of force can, in fact, be regarded as reasonable only if the particular circumstances warrant it. If the particular circumstances do not warrant the use of physical force, the use of **any** degree of force is unlawful. The degree of force employed must also be in proportion to the circumstances of the incident and the seriousness of the behaviour or consequences it is intended to prevent. Any force used should always be the **minimum** needed in order to achieve the desired result.

DfEE Circular 10/98:

- gives examples of circumstances in which physical intervention might be appropriate, and the factors that teachers should bear in mind when deciding whether to intervene;
- discusses the meaning of 'reasonable force';
- advises that schools should have a policy about the use of reasonable force, and should tell parents about it; and,
- advises that schools should record incidents in which force is used to control or restrain a pupil, and tell parents of any such incidents involving their child.

Section 550A of the Education Act 1997 contains the same information (quoted verbatim above) and it shows who may use reasonable force, when they may use it, and where they may use it. DfEE Circular 10/98 stresses the importance of schools having policies about the use of force to control or restrain pupils, and that parents and pupils be informed about what is acceptable and what is not.

DfEE Circular 10/98 gives examples of three fairly broad categories of situations in which reasonable force might be either appropriate or necessary to control or restrain: (1) where action is necessary in self-defence or because there is an imminent risk of injury; (2) where there is a developing risk of injury, or significant damage to property; and (3) where a pupil is behaving in a way that is compromising good order and discipline.

Situations falling within categories (1) & (2) are a pupil(s): (a) attacking a member of staff or another pupil; (b) fighting; (c) engaged in, or on the verge of committing, deliberate damage or vandalism to property; (d) causing, or at risk or causing, injury or damage by accident, by rough play, or by misuse of dangerous materials or objects; (e) running in corridors or on stairways in a way in which he or she might have, or cause, an accident likely to injure him or herself, or others; and (f) absconding from a class or trying to leave school (although this will only apply if a pupil could be at risk if not kept in the classroom or at school). Situations falling within category (3) are a pupil(s): (a) persistently refusing to obey an order to leave a classroom; and (b) behaving in a way that is seriously disrupting a lesson.

DfEE Circular 10/98 makes very clear that, whenever practicable, teachers should tell a misbehaving pupil(s) to stop and what will happen if they do not. A calm and measured approach to a situation is needed; teachers should never give the impression that they have lost their temper, or are acting out of anger or frustration, or to punish the pupil. The importance of always thinking and being prudent are stressed strongly and that, before any physical intervention, a teacher should always consider carefully if such intervention is necessary. Could other strategies be used? Are there better ways to defuse or calm the situation? Unless in a genuine emergency situation (such as stopping a young pupil running off the pavement onto a busy road), DfEE Circular 10/98 also indicates times when teachers should not intervene without help, such as dealing with an older or physically large pupil, or the teacher believes that he/she may be at risk of physical injury.

DfEE Circular 10/98 indicates the **acceptable** varieties of physical intervention in which teachers may be involved: physically interposing between pupils; blocking a pupil's path; holding, pushing or pulling; leading a pupil by the hand or arm; shepherding a pupil away by placing a hand in the centre of the back; or - only in extreme circumstances - using more restrictive holds.

Furthermore, DfEE Circular 10/98 warns of the sorts of physical intervention teachers should **not** employ because they might reasonably be expected to cause injury to the pupil. These are: holding a pupil around the neck, or by the collar, or in any way that might restrict the pupil's ability to breathe; slapping, punching or kicking a pupil; twisting or forcing limbs against a joint; tripping up a pupil; holding or pulling a pupil by the hair or ear; and holding a pupil face down on the ground. There is also a warning to avoid always touching or holding a pupil in a way that might be considered indecent.

DfEE Circular 10/98 also makes it quite clear that (except for minor or trivial incidents) a detailed, contemporaneous, written report should always be made on an occasion when physical force has been used. This could prevent any misunderstanding or misrepresentation of the incident, and it may be helpful should there be a subsequent complaint. Schools should keep an "Incident Book" for all such incidents and the Circular gives guidance on what reports in the Incident Book should normally include. Teachers should always inform the head teacher or a senior member of staff as quickly as possible, (and they might also consider whether or not they need to seek advice from their union). It should also be noted that the Circular points out that incidents involving the use of force can cause the parents of a pupil great distress and schools are advised to inform parents of any incidents involving their child, and give them an opportunity to discuss it.

16. "Working Together to Safeguard Children: a guide to inter-agency working to safeguard and promote the welfare of children", Department of Health/Home Office/Department for Education and Employment, 1999

(Readers should also see the chapter Protecting children from abuse: the role of the education service in the Protecting Children section of this booklet). The Children Act 1989 places two specific duties on agencies to co-operate in the interests of vulnerable children.

(1)   Section 27 of the Children Act provides that a local authority may request help from (amongst other authorities) any local education authority in exercising the local authority's functions under Part III of the Act. This part of the Act places a duty on local authorities to provide support and services for children in need, including children looked after by the local authority and those in secure accommodation. An authority whose help is requested in these circumstances has a duty to comply with the request, provided it is compatible with its other duties and functions. This, of course, means that, where applicable, individual schools in the local education authority must help the local authority when requested.

(2)   Section 47 of the Children Act places a duty on (amongst other authorities) any local education authority to help a local authority with its enquiries in cases where there is reasonable cause to suspect that a child is suffering, or is likely to suffer, significant harm. Again, this means that, where applicable, individual schools in the local education authority must help the local authority when requested. Section 47 of the Act is particularly important.

The Children Act 1989, Section 47(1) (b) states that:

Where a local authority –

(b)   have reasonable cause to suspect that a child who lives, or is found, in their area is suffering, or is likely to suffer, significant harm, the authority shall make, or cause to be made, such enquiries as they consider necessary to enable them to decide whether they should take any action to safeguard or promote the child's welfare.

The 1999 document *"Working Together to Safeguard Children"* describes how all agencies and professionals should work together to promote children's welfare and protect them from abuse and neglect. It is addressed to a variety of services, including the education service. The document (120 pages in length) contains a great deal of information and, for the sake of brevity, only the section concerning education services can be covered in this booklet. However, for a teacher who is the **designated teacher** within a school, a study of the complete document would be very wise. Under Education Services the document states:

3.10   All those working in the education services can contribute to the safeguarding of children and child protection processes. All schools and colleges have a pastoral responsibility towards their pupils. They can play a part in the prevention of abuse and neglect, through their own policies and procedures for safeguarding children, and through the curriculum. All schools and colleges should create and maintain a safe environment for children and young people, and should be able to manage situations where there are child welfare concerns. Children can be helped to understand what is and is not acceptable behaviour towards them, and taught about staying safe from harm, and how to speak up if they have worries or concerns. The curriculum can also play a preventive role in developing awareness and resilience and in preparing children and young people for their future responsibilities as adults, parents and citizens.

3.11   Through their day to day contact with pupils, and direct work with families, education staff have a crucial role to play in noticing indicators of possible abuse or neglect, and in referring concerns to the appropriate agency, normally the social services department. When a child has special educational needs, or is disabled, schools will have important information about the child's level of understanding and the most effective means of communicating with the child. They will also be well placed to give a view on the impact of treatment or intervention on the child's care or behaviour.

3.12   Staff working in the education service will on occasions be asked by a social services department for information on a child about whom there are concerns about abuse or neg-lect. The education service itself does not have a direct investigative responsibility in child protection work but schools and other maintained establishments have a role in assisting the social services department by referring concerns and providing information for s.47 (see above) child protection enquiries.

3.13   Where a child of school age is the subject of an inter-agency child protection plan, the school should be involved in the preparation of the plan. The school's role and responsibilities in contributing to actions to safeguard the child, and promote his or her welfare, should be clearly identified.

3.14   Throughout the education service:
• all staff should be alert to the signs of abuse and neg-lect, and know to whom they should report concerns or suspicions;
• all schools and colleges should have a designated member of staff with knowledge and skills in recognising and acting upon child protection concerns. He or she should act as a source of expertise and advice, and is responsible for co-ordinating action within the institution and liaising with other agencies.
• all schools and colleges should be aware of the child pro-tection procedures established by the Area Child Protec-tion Committee (ACPC) and, where appropriate, the Local Education Authority (LEA);
• all schools and colleges should have procedures for han-dling suspected cases of abuse, including procedures to be followed if a member of staff is accused of abuse;
• staff with designated responsibility for child protection should receive appropriate training;
• the school health service has a vital role to play in pro-

moting and maintaining the health of school children and in safeguarding and promoting their welfare;

• school governors should exercise their child protection responsibilities, in particular in response to allegations against headteachers, and in ensuring that there are school child protection policies in place;

• in every LEA a senior officer should be responsible for co-ordinating action on child protection issues across the Authority;

• all schools should have an effective who school policy against bullying and headteachers should have measures in place to prevent all forms of bullying among pupils;

• where a state school is concerned that a child may have 'disappeared', or about any aspect of a pupil transfer which gives rise to concerns about a child's welfare, it should report its concerns to a person specified in ACPC guidance, or to the LEA officer with designated responsibility for child protection;

• corporal punishment is outlawed for all pupils in all schools and colleges, including independent schools;

• teachers at a school are allowed to use reasonable force to control or restrain pupils under certain circumstances. Other people may also do so, in the same way as teachers, provided they have been authorised by the head teacher to have control or charge of pupils. All schools should have a policy about the use of force to control or restrain pupils.

The document *"Working Together to Safeguard Children"* shows the part that education services play in child protection matters is very important. No further explanation is required except to say that caring and vigilant teachers can play a crucial role in protecting children and young people from abuse and neglect.

Special Educational Needs/Disability

17. DfE Circular 9/94 and DH LAC (94) 9 "The Education of Children with Emotional and Behavioural Difficulties"

This Circular is discussed in the Protecting Children section of this booklet. However, in that context, the reference is to the physical restraint of pupils. In this section, the Circular's context is Special Educational Needs/Disability. The Circular was published jointly by the Department for Education (DfE) and the Department of Health (DH). Although over eight years old, the Circular is nevertheless still a very important guidance document.

The Circular is long (39 pages) and complex; it cannot, and it should not, be summarised in a few short paragraphs. It requires very careful reading and consideration. What the Circular does is to give guidance on good practice in the education of children with emotional and behavioural difficulties. It is intended primarily for local education authorities and schools; it is framed in the context of the Code of Practice on the Identification and Assessment of Special Educational Needs (SEN) and there is much overlap with the SEN Code of Practice and this Circular. (See the chapter dealing with the SEN Code of Practice in this section of this booklet.) The Circular also covers the important roles of parents, social services departments and health services.

"The Circular includes detailed advice on the early identification of emotional and behavioural difficulties in mainstream schools. Recording by schools is covered, with guidance on when further specialist advice is likely to be needed. Advice on provision in special schools is also given.

The second half of the Circular gives guidance to local education authorities on the use of residential schools. This stresses the crucial nature of early and effective liaison between the education and social services arms of the authority over place-

ment and funding. It includes criteria which may be used in
assessing the need for residential placements and guidance to
residential schools on their responsibilities.

The Circular also covers a number of other issues. These are
the involvement of health services with children needing psychiatric care; the particular needs of very young children and of
girls and young women; and the considerations which should
guide schools in exercising controls and sanctions over children
with emotional and behavioural difficulties."

The content of the Circular is structured under seven headings: (1) The
Scope of Emotional and Behavioural Difficulties and the Purpose of the
Circular; (2) School-based Provision and Assessment in Mainstream
Schools (Stages 1-3); (3) Subsequent Stages of Provision and Assessment
in Mainstream Schools (Stages 4-5); (4) Special Schools; (5) Residential
Provision for Pupils with Statements of SEN; (6) Children and Young
People Needing Psychiatric Care; and (7) Other Issues.

The Circular states that there are various definitions of emotional and
behavioural difficulties and that, for the purposes of the Circular, they lie
on the continuum between behaviour, which challenges teachers but is
within normal (albeit unacceptable) bounds, and behaviour which is
indicative of serious mental illness. The Circular makes clear that emotional and behavioural difficulties range from social maladaption to abnormal
emotional stresses. They are persistent (not necessarily permanent) and
constitute learning difficulties. They may be multiple and may manifest
themselves in different forms and severities. They may become apparent
through withdrawn, passive, depressive, aggressive or self-injurious ten-
dencies. They may have single or a number of causes and may be associated with school, family or other environments or physical or sensory
impairments. Children with these difficulties may be unable to trust or to
form relationships with peers or adults.

Children with emotional and behavioural difficulties cover the range
of ability found in mainstream schools and possess special educational
needs. Although dealing with such children can be difficult, schools must
deal with them because schools have responsibilities towards all their
pupils. Children with emotional and behavioural difficulties may present
themselves as challenges, of differing magnitudes, to the teacher's classroom control.

The Circular states that school governors have a duty to ensure that any
necessary special education provision is made in their schools; that the
special educational needs of pupils are made known to teachers; and that

teachers are aware of the importance identifying and providing for pupils' special educational needs as necessary. The school needs to give special attention to the academic progress of the child with emotional and behavioural difficulties, in particular to ways in which work can present a suitable level of challenge.

As the Executive Summary in the Circular states, *"Dealing with children with emotional and behavioural difficulties may be seen as an intractable and frustrating task for teachers. The difficulties are genuine. But emotional and behavioural difficulties are often engendered or worsened by the environment, including schools' or teachers' responses. Schools have a significant effect on children's behaviour, and vary widely in the extent to which they help children overcome their difficulties".*

The beneficial effect teachers can have is also spelt out *"Improvements in pupil behaviour are likely to follow if pupils' self-esteem is enhanced and if they are helped to recognise the effects of their behaviour. Teachers need to be constructive, and specific in terms of what is acceptable and what is expected".* Although the Circular is rather complex it is, however, a document that those completing courses of initial teacher training and Newly Qualified Teachers would do well to read carefully because they will soon be in situations where they will have to deal with children with emotional and behavioural difficulties.

18. DfEE and Department of Health Circular 14/96 "Supporting Pupils with Medical Needs in School"

This Circular, a joint DfEE/Department of Health publication, sets out the legal framework for mainstream school and local education authorities in supporting pupils with medical needs. The Circular also suggests that special schools, nursery schools and further education colleges may also find the guidance useful.

Circular 14/96:

1   summarises the main legal provisions that affect schools' responsibilities for managing a pupil's medical needs;
2   recommends schools draw up policies and procedures for supporting pupils with medical needs;
3   suggests health care plans, which include medication arrangements, are provided for pupils with medical needs.

Circular 14/96 points out that most schools are likely to have pupils with medical needs and, under Health and Safety at Work legislation, this may mean making special arrangements for these particular pupils. Furthermore, a Health Authority must, under Section 166 of the Education Act 1993, provide help to a local education authority, should it be required, for a pupil with special educational needs. Help from the Health Authority could include providing advice and training for school staff in procedures to deal with a pupil's medical needs if a pupil would otherwise have limited access to education. Authorities and schools need to work together, in partnership with parents, to ensure proper support for pupils with medical needs.

Under the Health and Safety at Work Act 1974, employers have a statutory duty for the health and safety of their employees and anyone else on the premises. In schools this includes pupils. Circular 14/96 makes the very important point that *"there is no legal or contractual duty on school staff* (and this, of course, includes teachers) *to administer a medicine or supervise a pupil taking it"* although, as the Circular points out, support staff may, as part of their contract, have specific duties to provide medical assistance. However, teachers and other staff in charge of pupils have a common law duty of care (see the Employment section of this booklet for information regarding common law duty of care). They must, therefore, act as any reasonably prudent parent would to make sure that pupils are healthy and safe whilst on the school premises. In exceptional circumstances this might extend to administering medicine and/or taking action in an emergency. The common law duty of care also extends to teachers leading activities taking place off the school site such as educational visits and field trips. It is well worth noting that Section 3(5) of the Children Act 1989 provides scope for teachers to do what is reasonable for the purpose of safeguarding or promoting children's welfare and this can give protection to teachers acting reasonably in emergency situations.

Circular 14/96 states that schools should have policies that are understood and accepted by staff, parents and pupils, and are a sound basis for ensuring that pupils with medical needs receive proper care and support at school. Children with medical needs have the same rights of admission to school as do other children and cannot, generally, be excluded for medical reasons. (See also the Special Education Needs and Disability Act 2001 in this section of the booklet.)

Those pupils who have a medical condition that, if not managed properly, could limit their access to education are regarded as having **medical needs**. Circular 14/96 states *"Most pupils with medical needs are able to attend school regularly and, with some support from the school, can take part in most normal school activities. However, school staff may need to take extra care in supervising some activities to make sure these pupils, and others, are not put at risk. In some cases, schools will find it helpful to draw up individual procedures, in the form of a health care plan, to ensure the safety of such pupils".* Obviously, the **health care plan** should be drawn up in conjunction with the parents and, where appropriate, the child and the child's medical carers. The plan should include preparation for any emergency situation. The information contained in an individual's health care plan must be treated in confidence and be used for no other purpose than for the school to set up a good support system.

To conclude this section it is worth restating what is written in the Employment section of this booklet (in the chapter dealing with aspects of the Health and Safety at Work Act 1974).

The administration of medication to pupils is not within the teachers' contract of employment and, normally, it is a pupil's parents who are responsible for their child's medication. There are very real dangers in a teacher deciding to give medication that has not been prescribed by a medical practitioner to a child. Teachers are not qualified medical practitioners and they do not know the full medical background of the child (such as the possibility of the child having an allergic reaction to a particular drug). Furthermore, teachers must not take the decision to administer even prescribed medication to a pupil(s), or give a pupil(s) permission to take medicine unless they are in situations such as an educational visit. In such a situation, the pupil's parents must (before the visit) provide the school with written details of what medication is required, the dosage, times of dosage, and their written consent for a teacher (or the pupil) to administer the medication. Local education authorities have very strict policies concerning the giving of medication and there is general information regarding medication, together with specific guidance on the control of asthma, epilepsy, diabetes and anaphylaxis in the DfEE good practice guide accompanying Circular 14/96 *"Supporting Pupils with Medical Needs in School"*.

19. The "Special Educational Needs Code of Practice", DfES 2001

This DfES 2001 publication is a book of 210 pages describing the new *Special Educational Needs Code of Practice* in great detail. Its focus, as the Secretary of State points out in the introduction, is on preventative work to ensure that children's special educational needs are identified as quickly as possible so that early action is taken to meet those needs. It also covers the special educational provisions of the Special Educational Needs and Disability Act 2001 (see also the description of this Act in this section of this booklet). The Special Educational Needs Code of Practice became effective in January 2002.

The *Special Educational Needs Code of Practice* defines what is meant and understood by the term "Special Educational Needs" by quoting Section 312 of the Education Act 1996:

> "Children have special educational needs if they have a **learning difficulty** which calls for **special educational provision** to be made for them.
>
> Children have a **learning difficulty** if they:

(a) have a significantly greater difficulty in learning than the majority of children of the same age; or

(b) have a disability which prevents or hinders them from making use of educational facilities of a kind generally provided for children of the same age in schools within the area of the local education authority

(c) are under compulsory school age and fall within the definition at (a) and (b) above or would do so if special educational provision was not made for them.

Children must not be regarded as having a learning difficulty solely because the language or form of language of their home is different from the language in which they will be taught.

Special educational provision means:

(a)   for children of two or over, education provision which is additional to, or otherwise different from, the educational provision made generally for children of their age in schools maintained by the local education authority, other than special schools, in the area

(b)   or children under two, educational provision of any kind."

There will be children with Special Educational Needs (SEN) in almost every school and **every school must have a written SEN Policy** presented in a parent-friendly format. The school's SEN Policy must be subject to a regular cycle of monitoring, evaluation and review.

  Schedule 1 of the *Education (Special Educational Needs) (Information) (England) Regulations 1999* states the basic information that is required concerning each maintained school's special education provision:

Basic information about the school's special educational provision

1.   The objectives of the governing body in making provision for pupils with special educational needs, and a description of how the governing body's special educational needs policy will contribute towards meeting those objectives.

2.   The name of the person who is responsible for co-ordinating the day to day provision of education for pupils with special educational needs at the school (whether or not the person is known as the SEN co-ordinator) (see description below).

3.   The arrangements which have been made for co-ordinating the provision of education for pupils with special educational needs at the school.

4.   The admission arrangements for pupils with special educational needs who do not have a statement (see description below) in so far as they differ from the arrangements for other pupils.

5.   The kinds of provision for special educational needs in which the school specialises and any special units.

6.   Facilities for pupils with special educational needs at the school including facilities which increase or assist accesses to the school by pupils who are disabled.

Information about the school's policies for the identification, assessment and provision for all pupils with special educational needs

7.   How resources are allocated to and amongst pupils with special educational needs.
8.   How pupils with special educational needs are identified and their needs determined and reviewed.
9.   Arrangements for providing access by pupils with special educational needs to a balanced and broadly based curriculum (including the National Curriculum).
10. How pupils with special educational needs engage in the activities of the school together with pupils who do not have special educational needs.
11. How the governing body evaluate the success of the education which is provided at the school to pupils with special educational needs.
12. Any arrangements made by the governing body relating to the treatment of complaints from parents of pupils with special educational needs concerning the provision made at the school.

Information about the school's staffing policies and partnership with bodies beyond the school.

13.   Any arrangement made by the governing body relating to in-service training for staff in relation to special educational needs.
14.   The use made of teachers and facilities from outside the school including links with support services for special educational needs.
15.   The role played by parents of pupils with special educational needs.
16.   Any links with other schools, including special school, and the provision made for the transition of pupils with special educational needs between schools or between the school and the next stage of life or education.

17. Links with child health services, social services and education-
      al welfare services and any voluntary organisations which
      work on behalf of children with special educational needs."

Schools have a statutory duty to identify all children with special educational needs and make proper educational provision for them. Within a
school, all teaching and non-teaching staff should be involved in the development of the school's Special Educational Needs Policy and they should
be fully aware of the school's procedures for identifying, assessing and
making provision for pupils with Special Educational Needs.

Many children with special educational needs have a **Statement of Special Educational Needs** outlining their needs and the special provision
required. The Education Act 1996 states that local education authorities
must identify and make a statutory assessment of those children for whom
they are responsible who have special educational needs and who probably
need a SEN statement. However, for a child who does not possess a statement of special educational needs, the Education Act 1996 also states that
schools have a statutory right to ask the local education authority to conduct a statutory assessment of a child's educational needs. Schools and
individual teachers, therefore, have a role to play in this process. The SEN
statement will (amongst other things) contain (i) details of all of the
child's special educational needs (learning difficulties) as identified by the
local education authority during the child's statutory assessment, and (ii)
the special educational provision that the local education authority considers necessary to meet the child's special educational needs. It is important
to note that many children with special educational needs do **not** possess a
SEN statement. However, schools, and individual teachers, must also provide for their particular educational needs.

Within individual schools, special educational needs provision falls
within one of two categories: (1) **School Action** and (2) **School Action
Plus,** these being the things that are done by a school to enable children to
access the National Curriculum when normal intervention does not succeed. Each of these terms are defined in the DfES 1999 *Special Educational
Needs Code of Practice.*

"School Action: when a class or subject teacher identify that a
pupil has special educational needs they provide interventions
that are additional to or different from those provided as part of
the school's usual differentiated curriculum offer and strategies.
An IEP (see description below) will usually be devised.
School Action Plus: when the class of subject teacher and the

SENCO (see description below) are provided with advice or support from outside specialists, so that alternative interventions additional or different strategies to those provided for the pupil through School Action can be put in place. The SENCO usually takes the lead although day-to-day provision continues to be the responsibility of the class or subject teacher."

An **Individual Education Plan** (IEP) is, as the *Special Educational Needs Code of Practice* states, *"a planning, teaching and reviewing tool. It is a working document for all teaching staff recording key short-term targets and strategies for an individual pupil that are **different from** or **additional to** those in place for the rest of the group or class."*

The *Special Educational Needs Code of Practice* states an Individual Education Plan should contain information about:

- The short-term targets set for or by the child
- The teaching strategies to be used
- The provision to be put in place
- When the plan is to be reviewed
- Success and/or exit criteria
- Outcomes (to be recorded when the IEP is reviewed).

Individual Education Plans should be reviewed at least twice a year and the SEN *Code* suggests that parents should be consulted as part of the review process and that parents' views on their child's progress should be sought. Furthermore, the individual pupils should also take part in the review process and be involved in setting the targets.

Although within individual schools, as the *Special Educational Needs Code of Practice* points out, provision for pupils with special educational needs is a matter for the school as a whole, the school's **Special Educational Needs Co-ordinator (SENCO)** (and, in secondary schools, the **SEN Team**) plays a key role. The SENCO takes day-to-day responsibility for the operation of the school's SEN Policy and the co-ordination of the provision made for individual children with special educational needs, working closely with school staff, parents, carers, and other agencies. The SENCO also provides related professional guidance to colleagues with the aim of securing high quality teaching for children with special educational needs. The key responsibilities of a SENCO are:

- overseeing the day-to-day operation of the school's SEN policy
- co-ordinating provision for pupils with special educational needs
- liaising with and advising fellow teachers
- managing the learning support assistants (and, in secondary schools, the SEN Team)
- overseeing the records on all pupils with special educational needs
- liaising with parents of pupils with special educational needs
- contributing to the in-service training of staff, and
- liaising with external agencies including the local education authority's support and educational psychology services, health and social services, voluntary bodies (and, in secondary schools, the Connexions Personal Advisers).

Within five pages, it has been impossible to provide more than a brief summary of some of the major features of special educational needs provision and what the 210-page DfES 2001 *Special Educational Needs Code of Practice* contains. Clearly a very great deal has, of necessity, been left out.

However, all teachers have a statutory duty to take account of the special educational needs policy of their school and to teach children possessing special educational needs. Furthermore, sooner or later, no matter what age range or subjects they teach, teachers will be involved in teaching children with special educational needs. It is, therefore, recommended that teachers familiarise themselves with the *Special Educational Needs Code of Practice* which is available, free of charge, from the DfES Publications Department (tel. 0845-602-2260).

20. The Special Educational Needs and Disability Act 2001

The Disability Discrimination Act 1995 was largely concerned with aspects of disability discrimination in employment and, in the Act, education was largely exempted from the Act's provisions (although certainly not as far as employers and employees' aspects of disability discrimination were concerned). However, the Special Educational Needs and Disability Act 2002 specifically extended the provision of the Disability Discrimination Act 1995 to education.

The Special Educational Needs and Disability Act 2002 was *"An Act to amend Part 4 of the Education Act 1996; to make further provision against discrimination, on grounds of disability, in schools and other educational establishments; and for connected purposes"*.

Part 2 of the Special Educational Needs and Disability Act 2001, Section 11, *Discrimination against disabled pupils and prospective pupils* states:

(1) It is unlawful for the body responsible for a school to discriminate against a disabled person –
(a) in the arrangements it makes for determining admission to the school as a pupil;
(b) in the terms on which it offers to admit him to the school as a pupil; or
(c) by refusing or deliberately omitting to accept an application for his admission to the school as a pupil.
(2) It is unlawful for the body responsible for a school to discriminate against a disabled pupil in the education or associated services provided for, or offered to, pupils at the school by that body.

Part 2 of the Special Educational Needs and Disability Act 2001, Section 13, *Disabled pupils not to be substantially disadvantaged* states:

(1)   The responsible body for a school must take such steps as it is reasonable for it to have to take to ensure that –
(a) in relation to the arrangements it makes for determining the admission of pupils to the school, disabled persons are not placed at a substantial disadvantage in comparison with persons who are not disabled; and
(b) in relation to education and associated services provided for, or offered to, pupils at the school by it, disabled pupils are not placed at a substantial disadvantage in comparison with pupils who are not disabled.

(2)   That does not require the responsible body to –
(a) remove or alter a physical feature (for example, one arising from the design or construction of the school premises or the location of resources): or
(b) provide auxiliary aids or services.

In the Special Educational Needs and Disability Act 2001, "Disabled Pupil" means a pupil who is a disabled person under the definition of the Disability Discrimination Act 1995 which states, *"A person has a disability for the purposes of this Act if he has a physical or mental impairment which has a substantial and long-term adverse effect on his ability to carry out normal day-to-day duties."* However, in the context of the Special Educational Needs and Disability Act 2001, the Children Act 1989 defines a "Disabled Child" as, *"A child is disabled if he is blind, deaf or dumb or suffers from a mental disorder of any kind or is substantially and permanently handicapped by illness, injury or congenital deformity or other such disability as may be prescribed"* and this is also relevant.

The provisions of the Special Educational Needs and Disability Act 2001 came into effect in September 2002. Since then, schools have been required not to treat disabled pupils less favourably for a reason relating to their disability and schools must take reasonable steps to ensure that disabled pupils are not placed at a substantial disadvantage to their peers who are not disabled.

Furthermore, the Special Educational Needs and Disability Act 2001 includes other important provisions that must be complied with. For example: (a) Part 1, Section 1 strengthens the rights of parents with a child with special educational needs to have their child educated in a mainstream school; (b) Part 1, Section 2 requires a local education authority to arrange for the parents of a child with special educational needs to be provided with advice and information about matters relating to those needs; and (c) Part 1, Section 7 provides that a local education authority or a school has a duty to inform parents where special educational needs provisions are made for a child.

The *Special Educational Needs Code of Practice*, DfES 2001 (discussed in the preceding chapter of this booklet) takes account of the Special Educational Needs (SEN) provisions of the Special Educational Needs and Disability Act 2001: (a) a stronger right for children with SEN to be educated at a mainstream school; (b) new duties on local education authorities to arrange for parents of children with SEN to be provided with services offering advice and information and a means of resolving disputes; (c) a new duty on schools to tell parents when they are making special educational provision for their child; and (d) a new right for schools to request a statutory assessment of a child.

The provisions of the Special Educational Needs Act 2001 are very important and they will have a considerable impact as time proceeds.

Inclusion and Discrimination

21. DfEe Circular 10/99 "Social inclusion: Pupil Support"

DfEE Circular 10/99 *"Social Inclusion: Pupil Support"* is an extremely important document. Governing bodies and head teachers must, by law, have regard to guidance contained in Circular 10/99. A key purpose of the guidance contained in Circular 10/99 is to help schools reduce the risk of disaffection among pupils and the Circular brings together guidance on all aspects of schools' pastoral and disciplinary policies. (The guidance must also be seen in the context of wider action, both nationally and locally, to prevent social exclusion such as supporting local communities, encouraging employment and reducing crime.)

Circular 10/99 (which is 66-pages long) explains the law and good practice on:

- pupil behaviour and discipline
- reducing the risk of disaffection
- school attendance and registration
- detention
- proper use of exclusion; and
- re-integration of excluded pupils.
  The emphasis is on early intervention and prevention through multi-agency working, and through partnership with parents.

Circular 10/99 points out that certain pupils are at particular risk. These include: those with special educational needs; children in the care of a local authority; minority ethnic children; Travellers; young carers; those from families under stress; and pregnant schoolgirls and teenage mothers. The particular problems and difficulties experienced by children in each of these groups are discussed. The Circular also points out that, for all pupils, transition from one stage of education to another requires particular care.

There are many indicators of disaffection in school and these can range from disruptive behaviour to unauthorised absence and prolonged truancy. Early intervention by the school, where there are signs of disaffection, may prevent problems from worsening. Circular 10/99 gives helpful advice on handling signs of disaffection. The value of the school working in partnership with the Careers Service, Education Welfare Officers and other agencies is discussed.

The problems of those pupils who do not respond the school actions to combat disaffection and who may be at serious risk of permanent exclusion or criminal activity, and may need a longer term intervention to keep them dropping out of school altogether, is discussed in Circular 10/99. Teachers should actively identify such pupils and each one will need a **Pastoral Support Programme** set up with external services as appropriate. The value of referring a pupil to a Pupil Referral Unit or a Learning Support Unit is discussed.

Circular 10/99 discusses, in considerable detail, the **use of exclusion**. Under Section 68 of the School Standards and Framework Act 1998, head teachers, school governors, local education authorities, and exclusion appeal panels must consider the guidance contained in DfEE Circular 10/99 when deciding:

- whether to exclude a pupil, for a fixed period or permanently;
- the length of the exclusion; and
- (where applicable) whether to direct the head teacher to re- instate an excluded pupil.

Circular 10/99 makes clear that a decision to exclude a child for a fixed period or permanently should be taken only:

- in response to serious breaches of a school's discipline policy; and
- once a range of alternative strategies (contained in Section 4 of the Circular "Handling signs of disaffection") have been tried and have failed; and
- if allowing the pupil to remain in school would seriously harm the education or welfare of the pupil or of others in the school.

Circular 10/99 contains examples of when exclusion is not appropriate (such as minor incidents, lateness, and breaching school uniform or hairstyle/jewellery policy). Because only head teachers can exclude pupils, individual teachers should take care never to threaten a child with exclusion.

Re-integration is also discussed in Circular 10/99. The successful integration of an excluded pupil is a challenge for both schools and pupils. Intensive local education authority support may well be necessary (including extra funding for the school) to help prevent a further exclusion. It is important to note that, for excluded primary pupils, *"The Secretary of State expects that most primary aged pupils excluded from school should be re-integrated with one term".* However, for pupils approaching the end of compulsory schooling, a return to school may well be unrealistic.

Circular 10/99 contains five important reference Annexes: Annex A *Guidance on attendance registers*; Annex B *The legal framework for school discipline*; Annex C *Detention: the law and how to apply it*; Annex D *Procedures for excluding a pupil*; and Annex E *School Reports to the Courts*.

22 "Education of Young People in Public Care" DfES 2001

This DfES Guidance document is 106 pages long and, therefore, only a brief outline of its contents can be given in this booklet. It is, however, available free of charge from the DfES Publications Department (Tel. 0845-602-2260).

The purpose of the Guidance document *"Education of Young People in Public Care"* is to assist local authorities in their role as corporate parents to safeguard and promote the education of children and young people in public care. It is intended to bring these young people's educational attainment closer in line to those of their peers, enabling them to achieve their full potential.

In 1999, the Department of Health's statistical analysis showed 55,300 children and young people being looked after by local authorities in England. 65% lived in foster placements and the rest lived in residential provision or with their families with social work support. Approximately 6,300 were looked after in children's homes. In recent years, the proportion of boys in care has risen, as has the number of younger children in care.

The document states, *"Children enter public care for a variety of reasons. Many have been affected by distressing and damaging experiences, including physical and sexual abuse and neglect. Some are in public care because of the illness or death of a parent or because their families in some way are unable to provide adequate care for them. The majority of young people in care come from families who experience hardship and are separated from them because of some form of family upheaval or breakdown. Less than two per cent of young people are in public care because of offences they have committed."*

The document makes it clear that young people's account of their experiences of care throw a very harsh light on the inclusiveness of services designed to meet their needs, including schools. The key factors concerning schools are identified as:

- children experience numerous, and often unplanned, moves of home;
- they experience unnecessary moves of school or are out of school for prolonged periods;
- making and sustaining relationships with peers an be particularly difficult due to lack of continuity in care and schooling;
- lack of continuity in care providers and teachers means that young people in public care cannot rely upon familiar adults who they trust to advocate for their needs;
- social services departments, LEAs and schools do not gather and share information that would help them to plan effectively;
- those responsible for the day-to-day care of young people in public care do not place sufficient value on education;
- schools and carers display lower expectations of young people in public care which can contribute to underachievement and failure;
- schools and social services do not act quickly and sensitively to help pupils in public care catch up when their education is disrupted;
- pupils in public care are over represented amongst pupils excluded from school;
- the special educational needs of some young people in care are not identified or addressed; and
- the needs of black and ethnic minority children are not always adequately considered in the care placement or educational placement.

Although there is a great deal of material of value for teachers throughout the document, the latter part of Section 5 is, possibly, the most useful. Paragraph 5.17 states, *"Every child and young person in public care needs a Personal Education Plan which ensures access to services and support; contributes to stability, minimises disruption and broken schooling; signals particular and special needs; establishes clear goals and acts as a record of progress and achievement."* A **Personal Education Plan** (as the document makes clear) should set clear objectives or targets for the young person which will relate to academic achievement as well as other personal and, if appropriate, behavioural targets, and details of who will action the plan with timescales for action and review. It will cover four areas: (1) **an achievement record** (academic or otherwise); (2) identification of **devel-**

opmental and educational needs (short and long term, development of skills, knowledge or subject areas and experiences); (3) **short-term targets** including progress monitoring; and (4) **long term plans and aspirations** (targets including progress, careers plans and aspirations). Furthermore, the Personal Education Plan should be an integral part of the individual's Care Plan and reflecting any existing education plans such as Individual Education Plan, Statement of Special Needs, etc.

It is suggested that there is a **designated teacher** in every school who understands about care and the impact of care upon education. A designated teacher in a school must have authority and is an important resource for the child, carers and parents, social workers, other teachers, school governors and support staff. He/she must be an advocate for the young people in public care, accessing services and support, and ensuring that the school shares and supports high expectations for them. The designated teacher should also ensure speedy transfer of educational information between agencies and individuals, and ensure that each child has a Personal Education Plan (see above) and that a Home/School Agreement is drawn up with the primary carer. Local education authorities should provide designated teachers with training.

It should always be remembered that the majority of children in public care will attend mainstream schools. These children in care, like their peers, should have full access to the National Curriculum and, as for other pupils, their achievement targets should relate to Key Stages. However, for some pupils, particularly older pupils, there may be a need for curricular flexibility to re-engage them or sustain them in education. For some, the school environment may be problematic or inappropriate and a blend of school, further education and work-related learning, in collaboration with the Careers Service, may be more suitable. (Since 1998, new flexibility was introduced allowing schools to set aside aspects of the National Curriculum at Key Stage 4 for individual pupils to undertake work-related learning programmes.)

The document also points out that approaches to learning and aspects of the curriculum can present difficulties for pupils whose life experiences are different from the majority of pupils. Such considerations must constantly be borne in mind by both schools and teachers in relation to race, gender, sexuality and disability. In particular, extra sensitivity is needed in dealing with aspects of the curriculum which deal with family values and experiences; these could rekindle distressing memories or put the spotlight on a child in public care.

Schools and teachers should always remember that some pupils live in poor families which are experiencing financial (or other) hardship. Schools should have sensitive arrangements for ensuring that – where additional resources are needed for a pupil to take part in a school or school-related activity (such as a geography field course) – help can be provided. Further- more, it is important that children in public care have access to study sup- port, including out of school hours support, to help them catch up with (or ensure they do not fall behind) their peers.

Finally, it must be remembered that, like their peers, children in public care may, at some time in their education, have special educational needs. (In fact, children in care are six to eight times more likely to have a State- ment of Special Educational Needs than pupils in the general school popu- lation.) However, it would be very wrong to assume that all children in public care have special educational needs. If a child in care does have spe- cial educational needs then these should be known to the school's Special Educational Needs Co-ordinator (SENCO), the school's Designated Teacher, their carer, and their social worker. The child's Personal Education Plan should detail their needs and the support already provided. Action should be taken according to the *Special Educational Needs Code of Practice* (see the chapter on this subject in the Special Educational Needs and Dis- ability section of this booklet).

23. The Disability Discrimination Act 1995, DfEE Circular 3/97 "What the Disability Discrimination Act 1995 means for Schools and LEAs" and the Special Educational Needs and Disability Act 2001

The Disability Discrimination Act 1995 is largely (although not entirely) aimed at preventing discrimination against disabled employees (and this is examined in the Employment section of this booklet). However, the Disability Discrimination Act 1995 also (a) makes provision for discrimination on grounds of disability when providing goods and services to disabled people and (b) requires school governors to publish information about the school's arrangements for disabled pupils. Thus, under the Act, governing bodies (and local education authorities) must also take account of: (a) any provision of non-educational services to the public, and (b) the arrangements for disabled pupils.

Although, under the Disability Discrimination Act 1995, the provision of education is excluded from the requirements, the provision of non-educational services is covered. "Service providers" (a "service provider" could be the school's governing body, a local education authority, a Parent Teacher Association, a local club that has hired premises from the school, etc.) must not discriminate against disabled people by:

- refusing to provide any service which is provided to members of the public;
- providing a lower standard of service or providing a service in a worse manner; or
- offering a service on less favourable terms.

DfEE Circular 3/97 states that this probably means activities such as:

- governing body meetings;
- services offered to pupils which are not related to their studies, such as skiing holidays;
- services offered to parents, such as governing body meetings to present the annual report;

- admission and exclusion appeal hearings where an appeal is by the parents;
- fund-raising events organised by Parent Teacher Associations such as jumble sales, boot sales or dances;
- leisure time activities for children or adults without any element of educational development; and
- the use of the school sports facilities by the local community or the hiring of school accommodation to members of the public;

come within the aegis of the DDA. Governors and LEAs must not unjustifiably discriminate against disabled people when providing non-educational services such as these.

Although, under the Disability Discrimination Act 1995, the first of the rights of access does not oblige service providers to make adjustments (such as to allow for wheelchair access or to provide a sign language interpreter for a parent who is hearing-impaired), school governors, local education authorities, etc., should take account of good practice and review their arrangements and take action to ensure that disabled people are not denied access to services.

Furthermore, under the provisions of the Disability Discrimination Act 1995, governing bodies **must** now publish in their annual reports to parents the following information:

- a description of the admission arrangements for pupils with disabilities;
- details of the steps taken to prevent pupils with disabilities from being treated less favourably that other pupils;
- details of facilities provided to assist access to the school by pupils with disabilities.

Finally, it is very important to note that DfEE Circular 3/97 *"What the Disability Discrimination Act (DDA) 1995 means for Schools and LEAs"* has now been discontinued by the DfES. This is probably because the Special Educational Needs and Disability Act 2001 (discussed at length in the Special Educational Needs and Disability section of this booklet) specifically added education to the Disability Discrimination Act 1995.

The Special Educational Needs and Disability Act 2001 is *"An Act to …* *make further provision against discrimination, on grounds of disability, in schools and other educational establishments".*

Part 2 of the Special Educational Needs and Disability Act 2001,

Section 11, *Discrimination against disabled pupils and prospective pupils* states:

(3) It is unlawful for the body responsible for a school to discriminate against a disabled person –

(d) in the arrangements it makes for determining admission to the school as a pupil;

(e) in the terms on which it offers to admit him to the school as a pupil; or

(f) by refusing or deliberately omitting to accept an application for his admission to the school as a pupil.

(4) It is unlawful for the body responsible for a school to discriminate against a disabled pupil in the education or associated services provided for, or offered to, pupils at the school by that body.

Part 2 of the Special Educational Needs and Disability Act 2001, Section 13, *Disabled pupils not to be substantially disadvantaged* states:

(3) The responsible body for a school must take such steps as it is reasonable for it to have to take to ensure that –

(c) in relation to the arrangements it makes for determining the admission of pupils to the school, disabled persons are not placed at a substantial disadvantage in comparison with persons who are not disabled; and

(d) in relation to education and associated services provided for, or offered to, pupils at the school by it, disabled pupils are not placed at a substantial disadvantage in comparison with pupils who are not disabled.

(4) That does not require the responsible body to –

(c) remove or alter a physical feature (for example, one arising from the design or construction of the school premises or the location of resources): or

(d) provide auxiliary aids or services.

Thus, it can be seen that the Disability Discrimination Act 1995 has been both extended and amended by the Special Educational Needs and Disability Act 2001. As far as education is concerned, the Disability Discrimination Act 1995 cannot, therefore, be considered in isolation and the provisions of the Special Educational Needs and Disability Act 2001must always be considered as well.

24. The Sex Discrimination Act 1975

The employment aspects of the Sex Discrimination Act 1975 are examined in the Employment section of this booklet (and, although it has been kept to a minimum, there is a certain amount of necessary repetition). However, the Act also affects schools and teachers in other ways and it is extremely important that teachers know of and understand them. Failure to observe the provisions of the Sex Discrimination Act 1975 could have serious consequences, as some teachers - often acting with the very best of intentions – have found out.

The Sex Discrimination Act 1975 renders unlawful (a) certain kinds of sex discrimination and (b) discrimination on the ground of marriage. Sex discrimination can be either direct or indirect and, in the definition of discrimination in the Act (the next paragraph), (a) is direct discrimination and (b) is indirect discrimination. The Act states:

1.- (1) A person discriminates against a woman in any circumstances relevant for the purposes of any provision of this Act if -

(c) on the ground of her sex he treats her less favourably than he treats, or would treat, a man; or

(d) he applies to her a requirement or condition which he applies or would apply equally to a man but -

(i) which is such that the proportion of women who can comply with it is considerably smaller than the proportion of men who can comply with it, and

(ii) which he cannot show to be justifiable irrespective of the sex of the person to whom it is applied, and

(iii) which is to her detriment because she cannot comply with it.

(2)   If a person treats or would treat a man differently according
       to the man's marital status, his treatment of a woman is for
       the purposes of subsection 1(a) to be compared to his treat-
       ment of a man having the like marital status.

it is essential to note the important fact that sex discrimination against
men is also unlawful under the Act and that the provisions of Section 1
*relating to sex discrimination against women are to be read as applying
equally to the treatment of men.* Furthermore, teachers should also take
note of the important fact that in the Sex Discrimination Act 1975,
"woman" includes a female of any age, and "man" includes a male of any age.
Children are therefore included and the Act, thus, has important implications for teachers. Teachers, therefore, must be aware of their own personal
responsibilities under the Sex Discrimination Act 1975 and ensure that
they do not infringe the provisions of the Act.

4.- (1) A person ("the discriminator") discriminates against another
        person ("the person victimised") in any circumstances rele-
        vant for the purposes of this Act if he treats the person vic-
        timised less favourably than in those circumstances he treats
        or would treat, other persons ....

Although teachers must be aware of their own personal responsibilities
under the Sex Discrimination Act 1975, educational establishments and/or
local education authorities, both as employers and in the ways that they
select and treat pupils (and teachers), also have particular responsibilities
under the Act. The Act (Part III Section 22) states that it is unlawful for an
educational establishment to discriminate against a woman -

(a)   in the terms on which it offers to admit her to the establish-
      ment as a pupil; or
(b)   by refusing or deliberately omitting to accept an application
      for her admission to the establishment as a pupil; or
(c)   where she is a pupil of the establishment -
      (i) in the way it affords her access to any benefits, facilities or
      services, or by refusing or deliberately omitting to afford her
      access to them; or
      (ii) by excluding her from the establishment or subjecting her
      to any other detriment.

Single-sex schools are exceptions and (a) and (b) (immediately above) do
not apply to them. However, schools that are co-educational must not have

an admissions policy, or any other practices, which are discriminatory under the terms of the Sex Discrimination Act 1975 and pupils must not be subjected to any forms of sex discrimination

In connection with this, the 1980s case of *Debell, Sevket and Teh – v - the London Borough of Bromley* has very important implications for co-educational schools. Michelle Debell, Selmin Sevket and Michelle Teh were all pupils at a primary school in Bromley. At the school, the children were grouped into classes by age and Class 10 was the top junior class for Year Six pupils (although Year Six was then termed fourth-year). In September 1982, the three girls, who were then (in age) Year Six pupils, all expected to enter Class 10. However, at assembly they were informed that all the Year Six boys with some Year Six girls would be going into Class 10, but that they and five other Year Six girls would be staying in Class 9 with Year Five pupils. When the girls' parents contacted the school they were told that there were too many children in Year Six for Class 10 (there were 39 children - 17 boys and 22 girls). However, they also discovered: (a) Class 10 had been organised to contain 17 boys and 14 girls; (b) no boys had been made to stay in Class 9; (c) Year Six boys younger than the three girls had been moved to Class 10; (d) the girls had not been kept in Class 9 because of lack of ability or aptitude; and that (e) the class division, contrary to the written policy of the school, had not been made on the basis of age alone but also on the basis of balancing the number of boys and girls in classes. Despite repeated requests by the girls' parents, the school and the local education authority refused to re-allocate the three girls from Class 9 to Class 10.

The girls' parents complained that, contrary to the Sex Discrimination Act 1975, their daughters who were (in age) Year Six pupils had been treated less favourably than boys who were Year Six pupils. Although a year later (in 1983), and acting on the advice of the Equal Opportunities Commission, the school arranged its classes on the basis of age alone, both the London Borough of Bromley and the head teacher refused to admit that their conduct in 1982 had been unlawful under the Sex Discrimination Act 1975 and they refused to compensate the girls. Legal proceedings were therefore commenced in the County Court. Eventually the London Borough of Bromley admitted that the acts, which the girls' parents had complained of, were unlawful breaches of the Sex Discrimination Act 1975 and a settlement was agreed. The implications of this case are very important; **schools must not attempt to achieve a sex balance in classes;** the guiding principle is that pupils must be treated on their individual merits, regardless of their sex. Furthermore, great care must also be taken not to fall foul of the Sex Discrimination Act 1975 through linking certain subjects to one particular sex (such as boys and woodwork or girls and cookery).

As can be seen from the above case, although teachers and schools each have responsibilities under the Sex Discrimination Act 1975, if an individual teacher discriminates against a pupil(s) then the legal principle of vicarious liability (see the Introduction to this booklet) can be applied and legal action could be taken against the individual teacher as well as against the school or local education authority.

Individual teachers have a personal responsibility to ensure that they do not participate in or practise - either inadvertently or on purpose - any form of sex discrimination and, thus, breach the sex discrimination legislation. Furthermore, in ensuring that they never subject a pupil(s) to any form of sex discrimination (either directly or indirectly), teachers must take care to **avoid practising positive sex discrimination**. This has sometimes been carried out both by establishments and individuals, often acting with the very best of intentions. However, just like negative discrimination, positive discrimination is also unlawful under the Sex Discrimination Act 1975. Teachers, therefore, must always be very careful how they treat pupils.

It is also well worth noting that, although different dress codes for males and females are allowed under the Sex Discrimination Act 1975, it is illegal if the dress code of one sex disadvantages the other. This particular issue received much public attention in 1999 when Dr Claire Hale challenged the legal right of Whickham School (a secondary school in Gateshead, Tyne and Wear) to enforce its school uniform policy.

At her primary school, Jo Hale (Dr Hale's daughter) and the other female pupils were allowed to wear trousers. However, Whickham School uniform regulations stipulated that girls had to wear the regulation skirt and they were not allowed to wear trousers. (Boys at Whickham School had to wear trousers.) In 1997/89 (her first winter at Whickham School) Jo Hale complained about feeling cold when wearing the compulsory school uniform skirt and Dr Hale wrote to the Headmaster asking him why trousers for female pupils were not included as an option in the Whickham School uniform policy. After discussions with the Headmaster and the Chairman of Governors, Dr Hale wrote a paper setting out her arguments in favour of letting girls wear trousers as part of the School's uniform policy. These were: practicality; warmth and comfort; cost; health and safety; personal safety; trousers being a uniform option for girls in other schools; and gender discrimination (under the Sex Discrimination Act 1975) with a uniform policy based on a stereotypical view of what was appropriate for girls. Although Dr Hale's paper was discussed at a meeting of the Whickham School Governors, the Governors refused to change the School's uniform policy.

Through her mother (because Jo Hale was under eighteen, Dr Hale had to act as her daughter's "litigation friend"), Jo Hale then served a questionnaire on the Whickham School Governors, under the provisions of the Sex Discrimination Act 1975, in which she expressed the view that the Governors may have discriminated against her because the School's uniform policy did not allow her to wear trousers and that, therefore, this was unlawful sex discrimination. The Governors replied that they did not believe the Whickham School uniform policy was discriminatory. The Equal Opportunities Commission (EOC) took up Jo Hale's case and the EOC asked Gateshead County Court to issue proceedings against Whickham School. The issue was, in fact, resolved before county court proceedings commenced. Whickham School Governors agreed to allow girls to wear trousers from Autumn 2002.

Hilary Slater (an Equal Opportunities Commission solicitor) commented, *"There is a strong argument that it is unlawful to prevent girls from wearing trousers to school now that trousers are an acceptable form of dress for women on virtually any occasion. I hope the settlement in Jo's case will persuade schools to review their uniform policies to eliminate unlawful sex discrimination".* Furthermore, it should be noted that when such discrimination cases do occur, some of them (such as the wearing of particular articles of clothing or jewellery) can also be linked to aspects of race relations. In addition, it is possible that such cases might also contravene Article 14 of the Human Rights Act 1998.

Although, under sex discrimination legislation, there is case law on dress codes in employment (see the case of *Schmidt –v- Austwicks Bookshops 1977*, in the chapter on the Sex Discrimination Act 1975 in the Employment section of this booklet) there is no such ruling on school dress codes for pupils. Because the Hale case was resolved before county court proceedings commenced, it did not provide a case law precedent on uniform/dress restrictions for pupils in schools. Hilary Slater also stated, *"The Equal Opportunities Commission continue to receive calls from people with questions on school uniforms and, while the legal argument for trousers is stronger as a result of this case, it is still not concrete.*

25. The Race Relations Act 1976 and the Race Relations (Amendment) Act 2000

The employment aspects of the Race Relations Act 1976 are examined in the Employment section of this booklet (and, although it has been kept to a minimum, there is a certain amount of necessary repetition). However, the Act also affects schools and teachers in other ways and it is extremely important that teachers know of and understand them. Failure to observe the provisions of the Race Relations Act 1976 could have serious consequences, as some teachers – often acting with the very best of intentions – have found out.

Individual teachers have responsibilities under the race relations legislation and they must take great care to ensure that their treatment of pupils is always non-discriminatory. This is a complex area and teachers must always ensure that both their behaviour and their actions are professional and within the law. If an individual teacher discriminates against a pupil(s) (under the Race Relations Act 1976) then the legal principle of vicarious liability (see the Introduction to this booklet) can be applied and legal action could be taken against the individual teacher as well as against the school or local education authority.

The Race Relations Act 1976 is concerned with (a) discrimination on racial grounds and (b) relations between people of different racial groups. Racial discrimination can be either direct or indirect. In the definition of discrimination in the Act (the following paragraph), (a) is direct discrimination and (b) is indirect discrimination. The Act states:

1.- (1) A person discriminates against another in any circumstances
     relevant for the purposes of any provision of this Act if –
   (c) on racial grounds he treats that other less favourably than
       he treats or would treat other persons; or
   (d) he applies to that other a requirement or condition which

he applies or would apply equally to persons not of the same racial group as that other, but –

(i) which is such that the proportion of persons of the same racial group as that other who can comply with it is considerably smaller than the proportion of persons not of that racial group who can comply with it; and

(ii) which he cannot show to be justifiable irrespective of the colour, race, nationality or ethnic or national origins of the person to whom it is applied; and

(iii) which is to the detriment of that other person because he cannot comply with it.

(2) It is hereby declared that, for the purposes of this Act, segregating a person from other persons on racial grounds is treating him less favourably than they are treated.

The Act defines the terms "racial grounds" and "racial group":

3.- (1) In this Act, unless the context otherwise requires –

"racial grounds" means any of the following grounds, namely colour, race, nationality or ethnic or national origins;

"racial group" means a group of persons defined by reference to colour, race, nationality or ethnic or national origins, and references to a person's racial group refer to any racial group into which he falls.

A landmark case of indirect racial discrimination [under (b) (i) above] with important and ongoing implications for schools, is that of *Mandla – v – Dowell-Lee (1983)*. Mr Mandla applied to send his son Gurinder to an independent school in Birmingham. The headmaster, Mr Dowell-Lee, imposed the condition on Gurinder's admission that he must cut his hair and conform to the school's rules on uniform; these precluded a turban. Being an orthodox Sikh, Mr Mandla felt unable to comply with these conditions and so he sent his son to another school where he could wear his turban. Mr Mandla (who was a solicitor) recognised an issue of legal principle under the Race Relations Act 1976 and he lodged a complaint of racial discrimination against the school. Although Mr Mandla lost in both the County Court and the Court of Appeal, the House of Lords reversed the Court of Appeal's decision and the Law Lords ruled that the school's refusal to admit the Sikh boy unless he renounced his turban amounted to unlawful discrimination. The Law Lords stated Sikhs were specifically entitled to the Act's protection, as they were an ethnic group. It should be noted that (with the exception of Northern Ireland) discrimination may be lawful on religious grounds and schools with a religious foundation may advertise for a teacher belonging to a particular faith. In the Mandla case, although Sikhs are a religious group, the Law Lords ruled in Mandla's favour because they decided that Sikhs were also an ethnic group and, thus, the headteacher was guilty of indirect racial discrimination under the Act.

Furthermore, in its publication "School Security: Dealing with Troublemakers" (1997), the DfEE pointed out that, although it is now an offence (under the Offensive Weapons Act 1996) to carry an offensive weapon or knife on school premises, Sikhs who have been initiated in a ceremony called Amrit Pahul are required to carry their kirpan (a ceremonial sword and one of the Sikh faith's five sacred symbols) at all times. The DfEE pointed out that although governing bodies and/or local education authorities must (under health and safety legislation) ensure the welfare of those within schools and satisfy themselves that the kirpan does not present a risk to either the wearer or to other pupils and staff, they must also be aware of the possible impact of the Race Relations Act 1976. Thus, the exclusion of a Sikh child who insisted on wearing their kirpan might well (as in the above case) be alleged to constitute unlawful indirect discrimination under the Race Relations Act 1976. It is quite clear that the case of *Mandla –v– Dowell-Lee (1983)* has long-lasting implications.

The Race Relations Act 1976 also incorporates specific legislation regarding racial discrimination by those in charge of educational establishments. Educational establishments and/or local education authorities, both as employers and in the way their pupils are selected and treated, have specific legal responsibilities under the Act.

Under Paragraph 17 of the Race Relations Act 1976, it is unlawful for an educational establishment to discriminate racially against any person:-

(a) in the terms on which it offers to admit him to the establishment as a pupil; or

(b by refusing or deliberately omitting to accept an application for his admission to the establishment as a pupil; or

(c) where he is a pupil of the establishment -
   (i) in the way it affords him access to any benefits, facilities or services, or by refusing or deliberately omitting to afford him access to them; or
   (ii) by excluding him from the establishment or subjecting him to any other detriment.

Clearly, educational establishments must have policies that are not in any way discriminatory (directly or indirectly) under the Race Relations Act 1976.

It should also be noted that racial discrimination can also be by way of victimisation. The Race Relations Act 1976 states:

2.- (1) A person ("the discriminator") discriminates against another person ("the person victimised") in any circumstances relevant for the purposes of any provision of this Act if he treats the person victimised less favourably than in those circumstances he treats or would treat other persons, ...

And, therefore, teachers must be careful never to victimise a pupil(s) on racial (or any other) grounds.

The Stephen Lawrence enquiry *("to enquire into the matters arising from the death of Stephen Lawrence")* was set up in July 1997 and the Inquiry's findings (the Macpherson Report) was published in February 1999. In the Macpherson Report it stated that, *"if racism is to be eliminated from our society there must be a co-ordinated effort to prevent its growth ... it is incumbent upon every institution to examine their policies and practices to guard against disadvantaging any section of our community."* The government, in its response, went considerably further than the Inquiry Report suggested and it extended and amended the Race Relations Act 1976 through the means of the Race Relations (Amendment) Act 2000.

The Race Relations (Amendment) Act 2000 extended protection against racial discrimination by "specified public authorities", and these include the governing bodies of educational establishments maintained by local education authorities. There is now a general obligatory duty requiring all specified public authorities to promote race equality. Schools (as a specified public authority), in everything that they do, now have a general statutory duty:

(c) to eliminate unlawful racial discrimination; and
(d) to promote equality of opportunity good relations between persons of different racial groups.

The Commission for Racial Equality is issuing six Codes of Practice, one specifically for educational bodies. Furthermore, in Chapter 6, paragraph 16 of a document from the Home Office discussing the Race Relations (Amendment) Act 2000, it stated (2001):

... we are proposing that each school in England and Wales should have specific duties to:

(d) prepare a **written policy** on race equality;
(e) **assess** the impact of its policies on ethnic minority pupils, staff and parents, with the emphasis on the attainment of ethnic minority pupils;
(f) **monitor** the levels of attainment of ethnic minority pupils, and the impact of the its race equality policy on pupils, staff and parents.

Quite clearly (and although there are aspects of the policy that apply to teachers as employees) the overall emphasis is on pupils. From now on, all schools will have to consider their race policies very carefully indeed and, in many cases, be more pro-active regarding maters of race than they have might been in the past.

Teachers must be sure they never subject a pupil(s) to any form of racial discrimination, either directly or indirectly and, thus breach race relations legislation. Furthermore, teachers must be careful not to practise positive discrimination. This has occasionally been carried out both by individuals and establishments, usually acting with the very best of intentions but is (just like negative discrimination) unlawful under the law. Teachers, therefore, must be very careful how they treat individual pupils and take care never to discriminate in either a negative or a positive way,

Although positive discrimination is unlawful, it is lawful to practise **positive action**. The Teacher Training Agency, for example, decided that the number of students from ethnic minority groups entering teacher training needed to be increased and positive action is being taken to ensure that ethnic minority groups are made aware of the fact that the government wants more ethnic minority teachers. This is lawful under the race relations legislation. However, if an educational establishment's admissions policy was to accept students from ethnic minority groups at the expense of other groups, then this would be unlawful because it would be positive discrimination.

26. The National Grid for Learning (NGfL) Inclusion Website

The National Grid for Learning (NGfL) website www.inclusion.ngfl. gov.uk is an Internet site that contains a catalogue of resources to support individual learning needs. The website is aimed at teaching professionals, learners, parents and carers. The resources *"include publications, software, hardware, guidance and links to other organisations to aid independent living and learning"*. The website can be used to:

- search for resources using the guided search or the quick search facility;
- view the most recently added resources;
- view case studies and comments on using resources; and
- access subject-based discussion groups.

Furthermore, if an individual has created or developed suitable resources, they can add those resources on line.

The National Grid for Learning Home Page has ten "buttons" with different titles (Home, Search, News, Sharing Practice, Legislation & Guidance, Discussion Groups, Help, Feedback, Add a Resource, and Alerting Service) that can be "clicked on".

For example: in *Legislation & Guidance,* the section has links to government legislation which has a bearing on meeting individual learning needs and there are links to both statutory and non-statutory guidance relevant to the provision of support to inclusive education. Two pieces of legislation (one an Act the other a Statutory Instrument) are listed: (i) the Special Educational Needs and Disability Act 2001, and (ii) the Special Educational Needs (Provision of Information by Local Education Authorities)(England) Regulations 2001. Two pieces of non-statutory guidance are listed: (i) Supporting Pupils with Medical Needs, and (ii) a General Statement on

Inclusion. A brief précis of what each piece of legislation/guidance involves is provided and, for each, there is a place on which to "click" for further information. For example: opening the *General Statement on Inclusion* brings up an outline page of how to view the three-part statement provided by the Qualifications and Curriculum Authority (QCA) aimed at teachers and Special Educational Needs Co-ordinators (SENCOs) setting out principles by which teachers can ensure all pupils have the chance to succeed.

The National Grid for Learning website is, clearly, an important Internet website that teachers (and others) can access. As time proceeds, and as more material is placed on the website, it will, undoubtedly become a very valuable resource indeed.

27 "Raising the Attainment of Minority Ethnic Pupils: School and LEA responses" (OFSTED 1999)

This 55-page publication (free from OFSTED) published the findings of OFSTED's inspection of the effectiveness of initiatives to raise the standards of minority ethnic pupils, especially those from Bangladeshi, Black Caribbean, Pakistani and Gypsy Traveller backgrounds. Evidence was also sought on what could be done to tackle problems of racial tension and harassment in schools. The document is substantial and only a few of the main findings and key issues can be provided in this booklet. However, teachers should read this OFSTED document which provides both encouraging and salutary reading.

The OFSTED inspection focused on four questions:

- What evidence do schools have on the relative performance of pupils from different ethnic groups?
- What strategies have schools implemented to raise the attainment of minority ethnic groups?
- What policies have schools developed for tackling stereotyping, ensuring high expectations and promoting good race relations?
- How do LEAs assist and work in partnership with schools to achieve successful outcomes in these three main areas?

The [edited] main findings the OFSTED inspection were:

The attainment of the minority ethnic groups

8   While the attainment of ethnic minority ethnic groups as a whole is improving, some groups continue to underachieve:
   • The performance of Bangladeshi and Pakistani pupils in the early years of school remains depressed. Once they become proficient in English, however, their attainment often match-

es or even surpasses that of English first language pupils in similar circumstances. Nevertheless, their generally lower attainment in higher grades at GCSE remains a concern.

• Black Caribbean pupils make a sound start in primary schools but their performance shows a marked decline at secondary level.

• Gypsy Traveller pupils are the group most at risk in the education system. Although some make a reasonably promising start in the primary school, by the time they reach secondary level their generally low attainment is a matter of serious concern.

• In general, girls from minority ethnic groups attain more highly than boys.

School initiatives

9   The majority of schools are engaged in a wide variety of initiatives to improve provision and raise the attainment of all pupils. However, few schools monitor these activities systematically and rarely do they have a specific ethnic focus.

10   Although most schools have equal opportunities policies, few have clear procedures for monitoring their implementation and their impact on practice is limited.

11   In the schools which have been most successful in raising the attainment of minority ethnic pupils, senior managers make clear that the under-performance of any group is not acceptable, gather evidence systematically and challenge individual teachers and departments to spell out what they intend to do to improve the situation.

12   Although schools record the numbers of pupils by ethnic group, the use of ethnic monitoring as part of a school's strategy for raising attainment has barely begun at primary level; too many schools are content to live with 'general impressions' or 'hunches' about the performance of different groups of pupils and these can serve to reinforce commonly held stereotypes.

13   Secondary schools are much more like to have attainment data analysis by ethnic group but few use this information as a key management tool for raising standards.

14   Very few schools review their curricular and pastoral strate-
       gies to ensure that they are sensitive to the ethnic groups in
       the student population and the wider community. In those
       instances where schools have done this as a result of con-
       cerns about a particular ethnic group, positive outcomes
       have resulted.

17   The schools in which minority ethnic pupils flourish under-
       stand the hostility these pupils often face (especially Gypsy
       Travellers). These schools have developed successful strate-
       gies for countering stereotyping which have not only had a
       tangible impact on the pupils' confidence and self-esteem,
       but have also influenced the attitudes of the majority.

18   An important feature of successful race relations work is a
       school ethos which is open and vigilant, in which pupils can
       talk about their concerns and share in the development of
       strategies for their resolution. This is true of both primary
       and secondary age pupils.

The OFSTED document also makes clear that many local education
authorities showed considerable weaknesses. For example, fewer than a
quarter of LEAs had a clear strategy for raising the attainment of minority
ethnic groups.

    The OFSTED document states the following **key issues** for schools and
LEAs.

24   To make sure that equal opportunities policies take effect,
       LEAs and schools must:
       • monitor pupil achievement and behaviour, including atten-
       dance and exclusions, by ethnic group;
       • use such data to:
            - set targets for raising the attainment and for improving
            the attendance and behaviour of underachieving groups;
            - manage and deploy grant-aided support more
            effectively;
       • monitor specific initiatives, such as the Literacy Strategy, to
       judge how well they are raising the achievement of all ethnic
       groups;
       • keep curricular and pastoral strategies under review to
       ensure they benefit all ethnic groups in the pupil population;
       • within the curriculum, give a clear priority to ensuring that

pupils from all ethnic groups make good progress and achieve high standards of literacy, numeracy and information technology;

• counter harassment and stereotyping by:

- stating clearly in policy documents that these are unacceptable attitudes and behaviours that will not be tolerated;

- creating an ethos in which these issues can be dis cussed openly by the whole school community including parents and pupils;

- giving practical advice on how to deal with racist behaviour.

25   In addition, LEAs have a duty to ensure that:

• Educational Development Plans (EDPs) address the needs of minority ethnic pupils;

• The role of the school link inspector with respect to equal opportunities is made clear;

• Training and advice to schools on the use of performance data to raise standards are available;

• The implementation of policies is monitored;

• Overall trends and patterns of performance are analysed by ethnicity;

• Good practice in raising attainment is disseminated.

28. "Evaluating Educational Inclusion: Guidance for inspectors and schools", (OFSTED 2000)

This 40-page document is not available in hard copy and it can only be obtained from the OFSTED website (www.ofsted.gov.uk). This OFSTED Guidance is aimed *"to help inspectors, and the governors and staff of schools, to identify what it means to be an inclusive school, and to diagnose the strengths and weaknesses of a school's practice in order to promote to bring about improvements in this area".*

The OFSTED document defines educationally inclusive schools as ones, *"in which the teaching and learning achievements, attitudes and well-being of every young person matter. Effective schools are educationally inclusive schools. This shows, not only in their performance, but also in their ethos and their willingness to offer new opportunities to pupils who may have experienced previous difficulties. This does not mean treating all pupils in the same way. Rather it involves taking account of pupils' varied life experiences and needs".*

The OFSTED document then goes on to state that, *"The most effective schools do not take educational inclusion for granted. They constantly monitor and evaluate the progress each pupil makes. They identify any pupils who may be missing out, difficult to engage, or feeling in some way to be apart from what the school seeks to provide. They take practical steps – in the classroom and beyond – to meet pupils' needs effectively and they promote tolerance and understanding in a diverse society".*

The statutory context makes it clear that schools (and inspectors) must have regard for:

1. the school's duties and obligations under existing legislation concerned with sex discrimination, race relations, special educational needs and disability discrimination;
2. ethical considerations related to values and social justice and

how the school promotes pupils' spiritual, moral, social and cultural development;

3. How well teachers promote the inclusive approach demanded by the National Curriculum when interpreting the educational objectives and courses provided;

4. Government policies aimed at raising educational standards, including: target setting by schools; promoting the inclusion of pupils with special needs or a disability; fostering better personal, community and race relations as highlighted in the [Stephen Lawrence Inquiry] Macpherson Report; and promoting social inclusion and race equality.

The OFSTED document is primarily written for school inspectors and, therefore, much of the specific detail is beyond what a Newly Qualified Teacher or student completing a course of initial teacher training would need to know. However, it is worth pointing out the questions concerning educational inclusion that an OFSTED inspector would be asking on his/her school inspection. These are:

•   Are all pupils achieving as much as they can, and deriving the maximum benefit, according to their individual needs, from what the school provides?

•   If not, which pupils or groups of pupils are not achieving as much as they can? Why not?

•   Is the school aware of these differences? If not, why not?

•   How does the school explain differences between groups of pupils in terms of achievement, teaching and learning and access to curricular opportunities? Are these explanations well founded and convincing?

•   What action (including use of nationally funded or local initiatives) has the school taken or is it taking to raise the standards of attainment of pupils or groups of pupils who appear to be underachieving or at particular risk? If none, why?

•   If the school is taking action, is it appropriate and is it effective or likely to be effective? Are there any unintended consequences? How well are these consequences being handled?

•   What action is being taken by the school to promote racial harmony, to prepare pupils for living in a diverse and increasingly inter-dependent society and specifically to prevent and address racism, sexism and other forms of discrimination?

It is also very well worth noting that the Stephen Lawrence Inquiry: Macpherson Report (1999) made several recommendations which the government accepted as duties on schools and their governing bodies, local education authorities, and OFSTED.

Recommendation 67
That consideration be given to amendment of the National Curriculum aimed at valuing cultural diversity and preventing racism, in order better to reflect the needs of a diverse society.

Recommendation 68
That Local Education Authorities and school Governors have the duty to create and implement strategies in their schools to prevent and address racism. Such strategies to include:

- that schools record all racist incidents
- that recorded incidents are reported to parents/guardians, school Governors and LEAs
- that the numbers and self defined ethnicity identity of "excluded" pupils are published annually on a school by school basis.

Recommendation 69
That OFSTED inspectors include examination of the implementation of such strategies.

There is, therefore, now a duty on all schools, regardless of the ethnic mix of the school's pupil population, to have strategies to prevent and address racism. There is also now a duty on OFSTED, through the inspection system, to monitor how effectively schools are implementing these strategies.

29 "Raising the Attainment of Minority Ethnic Pupils: Guidance and resource materials for providers of initial teacher training" Teacher Training Agency, 2000.

Many of those completing (or who have completed recently) courses of initial teacher training will know of this 118-page (free) publication from the Teacher Training Agency (TTA). This guidance document was produced in collaboration with the Commission for Racial Equality (CRE) and many other organisations and individuals (including teacher trainers and practising teachers). The aim of the guidance is to ensure that everyone involved in the training of new teachers is fully aware of their responsibility to equip their trainees with the knowledge, understanding and skills they need to raise the attainment of minority ethnic pupils and improve the quality of their education.

Although the Teacher Training Agency guidance document was not written for trainees, there is much in the TTA document that both trainees and practising teachers should be aware of. Because of space limitations, this booklet is not able to examine the TTA document in any detail and the reader is advised to obtain and peruse the document itself.

It should be pointed out that the Teacher Training Agency guidance document *"Raising the Attainment of Minority Ethnic Pupils"* was written with DfEE Circular 4/98 *"Requirements for All Courses of Initial Teacher Training"* in mind. DfEE Circular 4/98 has, however, now been superseded by the new 2002 DfES/TTA *"Standards for the Award of Qualified Teacher Status"* and, therefore, some of what is written in the document is out of date and no longer applicable.

After an introductory section, the Teacher Training Agency guidance document has ten main sections, nine of which relate to schools (Section 10 is concerned with good practice in the recruitment, retention and support of minority ethnic trainee teachers.) There is also a full bibliography and a useful list of contacts. In order to demonstrate the contents and breadth of the guidance document, a summary of the nine sections relating to schools is now provided.

Section 1 - *"including all pupils: setting the context"* which sets out the context for the guidance that follows later in the document.

Section 2 - *"the ethos and practice of the school"* which looks at some ways in which the ethos and practices of a school can affect the attainment of its pupils.

Section 3 - *"an inclusive curriculum"* which looks at the benefits of an inclusive curriculum in raising pupil attainment.

Section 4 - *"effective language and learning support for pupils for whom English is an additional language"* which looks at the importance of effective language and learning support in raising the attainment of pupils with English as an additional language (EAL).

Section 5 - *"understanding social, cultural and religious issues"* which explores some of the social, religious and cultural issues which can impact upon pupil achievement.

Section 6 - *"the early years"* - which looks at some issues which are particularly relevant to working with pupils in Early Years settings.

Section 7 - *"teaching refugee pupils"* - which looks at the particular needs of refugee pupils, and considers teaching methods and strategies to meet those needs.

Section 8 - *"effective liaison with parents and other carers"* - which considers some of the ways in which effective liaison with pupils' parents or carers can impact on the attainment and quality of education for pupils.

Section 9 - *"effective links between the school and the wider community"* - which considers how effective links between schools and the community they serve can impact on the attainment and quality of education for pupils.

It is, of course, quite impossible for this booklet to provide more than a flavour of what this very helpful guidance document contains and it is recommended that teachers obtain and read the Teacher Training Agency document *"Raising the Attainment of Minority Ethnic Pupils"* itself. The document, which is free, can be obtained from the TTA Publications Centre (0845-606-0323) and it can also be accessed on the TTA website (www.canteach.gov.uk).

Other Relevant Documents

30. DfEE Circular 10/98 "Section 550A of the Education Act 1996: The Use of force to Control or Restrain Pupils" and Detention of Pupils on Disciplinary Grounds (Section 5 of the Education Act 1997)

DfEE Circular 10/98 *"Section 550A of the Education Act 1996: The Use of force to Control or Restrain Pupils"* is discussed in this booklet's Protecting Children section. For clarity and ease of reference, what is written here repeats what is written elsewhere.

In the two earlier editions of this booklet (which were written to comply with the *"Other Professional Requirements"* requirements of DfEE Circular 4/98), the Detention of Pupils on Disciplinary Grounds was included. However, although this particular requirement is not shown in the DfES/TTA *2000 "Guidance on the Standards for the Award of Qualified Teacher Status"*, it is a subject which can cause teachers problems and, therefore, it has been included in this booklet.

Under the Education Act 1997, a teacher is permitted by law to use reasonable force to prevent pupils: committing offences; causing personal injury to, or damage to the property of another person (including the pupil); and engaging in forms of behaviour that are prejudicial to the maintenance of good order and discipline at the school. Teachers are also permitted to take restraining action both on the school premises and when they have lawful control (such as on a field trip). **However, they should always be mindful of the possibility of a subsequent claim of assault so they should act with utmost prudence and use only the minimum necessary force.**

By adding Section 550A to the Education Act 1996, the Education Act 1997 clarified the position concerning the use of physical force by teachers to control or restrain pupils. This came into force on 1 September 1998 and applies to all schools. The definitive guidance document is now DfEE Circular 10/98 *"Section 550A of the Education Act: The Use of force to Control or Retrain Pupils"* and all teachers and schools must follow these guidelines.

DfEE Circular 10/98 points out that, since the Children Act 1989, there has been a common misconception that any physical contact with a child is unlawful but that belief is not correct. Where necessary, reasonable force can be used to control or to restrain pupils. However, Circular 10/98 makes it clear there is no legal definition of "reasonable force" and that it will always depend on all the circumstances of the particular case. The use of force can, in fact, be regarded as reasonable only if the particular circumstances warrant it. If the particular circumstances do not warrant the use of physical force, the use of **any** degree of force is unlawful. The degree of force employed must also be in proportion to the circumstances of the incident and the seriousness of the behaviour or consequences it is intended to prevent. Any force used should always be the **minimum** needed in order to achieve the desired result.

DfEE Circular 10/98:

- gives examples of circumstances in which physical intervention might be appropriate, and the factors that teachers should bear in mind when deciding whether to intervene;
- discusses the meaning of 'reasonable force';
- advises that schools should have a policy about the use of reasonable force, and should tell parents about it; and,
- advises that schools should record incidents in which force is used to control or restrain a pupil, and tell parents of any such incidents involving their child.

Section 550A of the Education Act 1997 contains the same information (quoted verbatim above) and it shows who may use reasonable force, when they may use it, and where they may use it. DfEE Circular 10/98 stresses the importance of schools having policies about the use of force to control or restrain pupils, and that parents and pupils be informed about what is acceptable and what is not.

DfEE Circular 10/98 gives examples of three fairly broad categories of situations in which reasonable force might be either appropriate or necessary to control or restrain: (1) where action is necessary in self-defence or because there is an imminent risk of injury; (2) where there is a developing risk of injury, or significant damage to property; and (3) where a pupil is behaving in a way that is compromising good order and discipline.

Situations falling within categories (1) & (2) are a pupil(s): (a) attacking a member of staff or another pupil; (b) fighting; (c) engaged in, or on the verge of committing, deliberate damage or vandalism to property; (d) causing, or at risk or causing, injury or damage by accident, by rough play, or by misuse of dangerous materials or objects; (e) running in corridors or on stairways in a way in which he or she might have, or cause, an accident likely to injure him or herself, or others; and (f) absconding from a class or trying to leave school (although this will only apply if a pupil could be at risk if not kept in the classroom or at school). Situations falling within category (3) are a pupil(s): (a) persistently refusing to obey an order to leave a classroom; and (b) behaving in a way that is seriously disrupting a lesson.

DfEE Circular 10/98 makes very clear that, whenever practicable, teachers should tell a misbehaving pupil(s) to stop and what will happen if they do not. A calm and measured approach to a situation is needed; teachers should never give the impression that they have lost their temper, or are acting out of anger or frustration, or to punish the pupil. The importance of always thinking and being prudent are stressed strongly and that, before any physical intervention, a teacher should always consider carefully if such intervention is necessary. Could other strategies be used? Are there better ways to defuse or calm the situation? Unless in a genuine emergency situation (such as stopping a young pupil running off the pavement onto a busy road), DfEE Circular 10/98 also indicates times when teachers should not intervene without help, such as dealing with an older or physically large pupil, or the teacher believes that he/she may be at risk of physical injury.

DfEE Circular 10/98 indicates the **acceptable** varieties of physical intervention in which teachers may be involved: physically interposing between pupils; blocking a pupil's path; holding, pushing or pulling; leading a pupil by the hand or arm; shepherding a pupil away by placing a hand in the centre of the back; or - only in extreme circumstances - using more restrictive holds.

Furthermore, DfEE Circular 10/98 warns of the sorts of physical intervention teachers should **not** employ because they might reasonably be expected to cause injury to the pupil. These are: holding a pupil around the neck, or by the collar, or in any way that might restrict the pupil's ability to breathe; slapping, punching or kicking a pupil; twisting or forcing limbs against a joint; tripping up a pupil; holding or pulling a pupil by the hair or ear; and holding a pupil face down on the ground. There is also the warning to avoid always touching or holding a pupil in a way that might be considered indecent.

DfEE Circular 10/98 also makes it quite clear that (except for minor or trivial incidents) a detailed, contemporaneous, written report should always be made on an occasion when physical force has been used. This could prevent any misunderstanding or misrepresentation of the incident, and it may be helpful should there be a subsequent complaint. Schools should keep an "Incident Book" for all such incidents and the Circular gives guidance on what reports in the Incident Book should normally include. Teachers should always inform the head teacher or a senior member of staff as quickly as possible, (and they might also consider whether or not they need to seek advice from their union.) It should also be noted that the Circular points out that incidents involving the use of force can cause the parents of a pupil great distress and schools are advised to inform parents of any incidents involving their child, and give them an opportunity to discuss it.

In most schools, pupils who commit misdemeanours are usually given punishments. The Education Act 1966 (section 548) makes clear, members of staff in maintained schools no longer have the authority or right to give corporal punishment. Corporal punishment is forbidden and unlawful and is now gross misconduct for which a teacher can be dismissed immediately. Furthermore, the use of corporal punishment may also result in criminal proceedings in the courts. Therefore, other forms of punishment have to be used and one such punishment, frequently employed by schools, is the "detention". This can take various forms and a detention can take place during the school day (such as missing a playtime) or outside school hours. In the case of detentions which take place after the school day has ended, it is necessary to give a child's parents at least twenty four hours notice of the detention so the parents know that their child will be late and so that they can, if/where appropriate, make any necessary travelling arrangements.

Most parents are willing to accept the fact that their child must take part in a detention outside school hours if the child has committed a misdemeanour at school and the detention is justified on disciplinary grounds. Although parents must have at least 24 hours' written warning, and although it is clearly gratifying if they do give their consent, it is not legally necessary to obtain their permission. Section 5 of the Education Act 1997 states that detention outside of school hours is lawful despite absence of parental consent. However, certain conditions must always be satisfied. Section 5 of the Education Act 1997 states:

(1)   Where a pupil to whom this section applies is required on disciplinary grounds to spend a period of time in detention at his school after the end of any school session, his detention shall not be rendered unlawful by virtue of the absence of his parents' consent to it if the conditions set out in subsection (3) are satisfied.

(2)   This section applies to any pupil who has not attained the age of 18 and is attending –
(a) a school maintained by a local education authority;
(b) a grant-maintained or a grant-maintained special school; or
(c) a city technology college or city college for technology or the arts.

(3)   The conditions referred to in subsection (1) are as follows –
(a) the head teacher of the school must have previously determined, and have –
　　(i) made generally known within the school, and
　　(ii) taken steps to bring to the attention of the parent of every person who is for the time being a registered pupil there,
　　that the detention of pupils after the end of a school session is one of the measures that may be taken with a view to regulating the conduct of pupils;
(b) the detention must be imposed by the head teacher or by another teacher at the school specifically or generally authorised by him for the purpose;
(c) the detention must be reasonable in all the circumstances and
(d) the pupil's parent must have been given at least 24 hours' notice in writing that the detention was due to take place.

(4)   In determining for the purposes of subsection (3)(c) whether a pupil's detention is reasonable, the following matters in particular shall be taken into account -
(a) whether the detention constitutes a proportionate punishment in the circumstances of the case; and
(b) any special circumstances relevant to its imposition on the pupil which are known to the person imposing it (or of which he ought reasonably to be aware) including in particular –
　　(i) the pupil's age,
　　(ii) any special educational needs he may have,
　　(iii) any religious requirements affecting him, and
　　(iv) where arrangements have to be made for him to travel from the school to his home, whether suitable alternative arrangements can reasonably be made by his parent.

(5)   Section 572 [of the Education Act 1966], which provides for the methods [see following paragraph] by which notices may be served under this Act, does not preclude a notice from being given to a pupil's parent under this section by any other effective method.

The methods by which such notices must be given to parents are -

(a)   delivering it to that person, or
(b)   by leaving it at his usual or last known place of residence, or
(c)   by sending it in a prepaid letter addressed to him at that place.

In summary, under the Education Act 1997, maintained schools may lawfully hold detentions after school hours, despite the absence of parental consent, providing that: (a) all parents are aware of the fact that the detention of pupils after school hours is one of the measures that the school can take; (b) in the particular circumstances, the detention constitutes a reasonable punishment; (c) the head (or the authorised teacher) imposes the detention; (d) the pupil's parents have been given at least twenty four hours' notice, in writing, of the detention; and (e) all special circumstances (such as religious requirements or any transport arrangements) relevant to the imposition of the detention on a pupil have been taken fully into account. Providing a teacher's actions accord with these requirements, then the Education Act 1997 will support them if they give a pupil a detention.

However, a word of caution is necessary about imposing **blanket detentions** and the case of *Terrington – v - Lancashire County Council (1986)*, where a parent sued for false imprisonment of his son, should be noted. Here a teacher imposed a blanket detention on a whole class (so that he could establish sound discipline at the beginning of the school year) after continuous disruptions to his lesson and despite several warnings; the whole class of 25 pupils was detained for merely ten minutes. Although, on hearing the evidence, the Registrar gave judgement for Lancashire County Council, the parent appealed contending that the punishment was not reasonable because his son was innocent of causing disruption and, therefore, a blanket detention was unreasonable. Although the appeal judge found for Lancashire County Council, his words concerning blanket detentions should be noted: *"Punishment should not be indiscriminate. A blanket punishment such as detention of a whole class must only be used as a last resort, otherwise people who are quite innocent may be detained incorrectly or unlawfully."* Furthermore, in its report *"Discipline in Schools: Report of the Committee of Enquiry Chaired by Lord Elton"* (1989), the Elton Committee recommended avoidance of the punishment of whole groups of pupils.

Punishment must, therefore, relate to an individual pupil. The mass punishment of a group - particularly in cases where individual offenders or perpetrators cannot be identified - is likely to be regarded as a breach of the European Convention on Human Rights and the Human Rights Act 1998 (see the chapter dealing with the Human Rights Act 1998 in this booklet). Quite clearly, blanket detentions are things that teachers should, at all costs, avoid threatening or imposing.

31. The General Teaching Council & the "Code of Professional Values and Practice for Teachers"

In each of the eight parts of Section 1 (Professional Values and Practice) of *Standards for the Award of Qualified Teacher Status*, reference is made to the Professional Code of the General Teaching Council for England (hereafter referred to as the GTC). It is, therefore, important to reproduce the GTC Code in full. (Further information concerning the GTC and what it means for teachers can be found in the last section of this booklet.)

The GTC Code was drawn up following an extensive consultation with teachers. The GTC's original draft Code was modified in the light of the many consultation responses to reflect the context in which teachers work and the principles that govern how teachers relate to pupils, colleagues, other professionals, parents and carers and to the wider community. The Code also affirms that teachers develop and enhance their skills to ensure high quality teaching and learning.

It is worth noting the fact that, of the 20,000 teachers who responded to the consultation, 77% agreed or agreed strongly that the Code provided a useful summary of the beliefs, values and attitudes of the members of the teaching profession, and 68% agreed or agreed strongly that the Code provided useful general guidance for teachers. The teachers also told the GTC that they would welcome a statement affirming the high standards that exist in the profession and also said that a Code that articulated the beliefs, values and attitudes that make up teacher professionalism would be valuable and helpful in raising the morale of the teacher profession.

The GTC formally agreed the Code of Professional Values and Practice for Teachers in February 2002

Code of Professional Values and Practice for Teachers
General introduction: the high standards of the teaching profession

Teachers inspire and lead young people, helping them achieve their potential as fulfilled individuals and productive members of society. Their role is vital, unique and far-reaching.

This Code sets out the beliefs, values and attitudes that make up teacher professionalism. It shows that teachers use high levels of individual judgement and skill to meet the challenges of their profession.

It recognises that teachers work within a framework of legislation with many lines of accountability. The complicated and varied roles that teachers need to fulfil make teaching one of the most demanding and rewarding professions.

Many of those who enter the profession feel a strong sense of vocation in accepting the special challenge of teaching and its chances to improve the opportunities that young people have in life. First and foremost, teachers are competent classroom practitioners. The role of teachers is to achieve success for their pupils through a complex network of relationships. They need high levels of commitment, energy and enthusiasm. Like other professionals, teachers respond to a social situation that is continually changing.

To ensure the positive development of individual pupils, teachers work within a framework of equal opportunities and other relevant legislation, statutory guidance and school policies. Within this framework, teachers challenge stereotypes and oppose prejudice to safeguard equality of opportunity, respecting individuals regardless of gender, marital status, religion, colour, race, ethnicity, class, sexual orientation, disability and age.

We produced this Code after wide consultation, to confirm the values and high standards of professional practice by teachers. As such, it forms the basis of all the Council's advisory and regulatory work. We are carrying out work to develop notes of guidance in the areas covered in this Code as well as a Code of Conduct for use in our regulatory role.

Professionalism in practice

Young people as pupils

Teachers have insight into the learning needs of young people. They use professional judgement to meet those needs and to choose the best ways of motivating pupils to achieve success. They use assessment to inform and guide their work.

Teachers have high expectations for all pupils, helping them progress regardless of their personal circumstances and different needs and backgrounds. They work to make sure that pupils develop intellectually and personally, and to safeguard pupils' general health, safety and well-being. Teachers demonstrate the characteristics they are trying to inspire in pupils, including a spirit of intellectual enquiry, tolerance, honesty, fairness, patience, a genuine concern for other people and an appreciation of different backgrounds.

Teacher Colleagues

Teachers support their colleagues in achieving the highest professional standards. They are fully committed to sharing their own expertise and insights in the interests of the people they teach and are always open to learning from the effective practice of their colleagues. Teachers respect the rights of other people to equal opportunities and to dignity at work. They respect confidentiality where appropriate.

Other professionals, governors and interested people

Teachers recognise that the well-being and development of pupils often depend on working in partnership with different professionals, the school governing body, support staff and other interested people within and beyond the school. They respect the skills, expertise and contributions of these colleagues and partners and are concerned to build productive working relationships with them in the interests of pupils.

Parents and carers

Teachers respond sensitively to the differences in pupils' home backgrounds and circumstances and recognise the importance of working in partnership with parents and carers to understand and support their children's learning. They endeavour to communicate effectively and promote co-operation between the home and the school for the benefit of young people.

The school in context

Teachers support the place of the school in the community and appreciate the importance of their own professional status in society. They recognise that professionalism involves using judgement over appropriate standards of personal behaviour.

Learning and development

Teachers entering the teaching profession in England have been trained to a professional standard that has prepared them for the rigours and realities of the classroom. They understand that maintaining and developing their skills, knowledge and expertise is vital to achieving success. They take responsibility for their own continuing professional development, through the opportunities available to them, to make sure that pupils receive the best and most relevant education. Teachers continually reflect on their own practice, improve their skills and deepen their knowledge. They want to adapt their teaching appropriately to take account of new findings, ideas and technologies.

Conclusion

This Code is intended to help make sure that the professional work of teachers helps their pupils to develop themselves fully and reach their highest potential in life. It is intended to be an evolving document that will contribute to the definition of teacher professionalism and help in raising standards of achievement by pupils.

32. Sections 548, 550A & 572 of the Education Act 1996, and Section 4 of the Education Act 1997.

Sections 548, 550A & 572 of the Education Act 1996 and Section 4 of the Education Act 1997are dealt with fully in other parts of this booklet and it is not proposed to devote more than a few lines to each of the four sections.

Section 548 of the Education Act 1996 concerns **corporal punishment** and it states that members of staff in maintained schools no longer have the authority or the right to give corporal punishment. Corporal punishment is forbidden and unlawful. Corporal punishment is classed as gross misconduct for which a teacher can be dismissed immediately and, furthermore, the use of corporal punishment may result in criminal proceedings in the courts.

In this booklet, this is covered fully in:

- the Employment section in the chapter titled *Appropriate Physical Restraint of Pupils (Section 4 of the Education Act 1997, DfE Circular 9/94 and DH LAC (94) 9 "The Education of Children with Emotional and Behavioural Difficulties" and DfEE Circular 10/98 "Section 550A of the Education Act 1996: The Use of force to Control or Restrain Pupils");* and
- the Other Relevant Documents section in the chapter titled *DfEE Circular 10/98 "Section 550A of the Education Act 1996: The Use of force to Control or Restrain Pupils" and Detention of Pupils on Disciplinary Grounds (Section 5 Of the Education Act 1997).*

Section 550A of the Education Act 1996 concerns the **use of reasonable force to control or restrain pupils** and it clarifies the powers of teachers (and other school staff who have lawful control or charge of pupils) to use reasonable force to prevent pupils: committing a crime; causing injury or damage; or causing disruption.

In this booklet, this is fully covered in:

- the Employment section in the chapter titled *Appropriate Physical Restraint of Pupils (Section 4 of the Education Act 1997, DfE Circular 9/94 and DH LAC (94) 9 "The Education of Children with Emotional and Behavioural Difficulties" and DfEE Circular 10/98 "Section 550A of the Education Act 1996: The Use of force to Control or Restrain Pupils");* and
- the Other Relevant Documents section in the chapter titled *DfEE Circular 10/98 "Section 550A of the Education Act 1996: The Use of force to Control or Restrain Pupils" and Detention of Pupils on Disciplinary Grounds (Section 5 Of the Education Act 1997).*

Section 572 of the Education Act 1996 concerns the giving of **detentions** and it states the methods by which detention notices may be served (although it does not preclude a notice from being given to a pupil's parent by any other effective method). The methods are: (a) delivering it to that person; (b) by leaving it at his usual or last known place of residence, or (c) or sending it in a prepaid letter addressed to him at that place.

In this booklet, this is fully covered in:

- the Other Relevant Documents section in the chapter titled DfEE Circular 10/98 *"Section 550A of the Education Act 1996: The Use of force to Control or Restrain Pupils"* and Detention of Pupils on Disciplinary Grounds (Section 5 Of the Education Act 1997).

Section 4 of the Education Act 1997 also deals with the **appropriate physical restraint of pupils.** Basically, a member of staff of a school may use, in relation to any pupil at the school, such force as is reasonable in the circumstances for the purpose of preventing the pupil from: committing any offence; causing personal injury to, or damage to the property of, any person (including the pupil himself), or engaging in any behaviour prejudicial to the maintenance of good order and discipline at the school or among any of its pupils, whether that behaviour occurs during a teaching lesson or otherwise. This applies where a member of the staff of a school is on the premises of the school or elsewhere at a time when, as a member of its staff, he has lawful control or charge of the pupil concerned. However, it does not authorise anything to be done in relation to a pupil which constitutes the giving of corporal punishment within the meaning of section 548 of the Education Act 1996.

In this booklet, this is fully covered in:

- the Employment section in the chapter titled *Appropriate Physical Restraint of Pupils (Section 4 of the Education Act 1997, DfE Circular 9/94 and DH LAC (94) 9 "The Education of Children with Emotional and Behavioural Difficulties" and DfEE Circular 10/98 "Section 550A of the Education Act 1996: The Use of force to Control or Restrain Pupils").*

33. The Human Rights Act 1998

The Human Rights Act 1998 is *"an Act to give further effect to rights and freedoms guaranteed under the European Convention on Human Rights".* The Act 1998 came into force in October 2000. The Home Office booklet *"Human Rights Act: an introduction" (2000)* makes clear that the Act:

- makes it unlawful for a "public authority", like a government department, local authority or the police, to breach the Convention Rights, unless an Act of Parliament meant it could not have acted differently;
- means that cases (that previously had to go to the European Court of Human Rights in Strasbourg) can now be dealt with in a United Kingdom court or tribunal; and
- says that all United Kingdom legislation must be given a meaning that fits with the Convention rights, if that is possible.

Under the Human Rights 0Act 1998, the governing bodies of all maintained and (probably) independent schools count as "public authorities" and nothing that a governing body does should contravene the European Convention on Human Rights.

The Human Rights Act 1998 contains sixteen basic "Rights", all taken from the European Convention on Human Rights. The area of the Act most relevant to schools is Protocol 1, Article 2, the "Right to Education". This states that, *"No person shall be denied the right to education".* In the Home Office *"Study Guide (to) the Human Rights Act 1998",* the individual's rights to education are spelt out.

PROTOCOL 1, ARTICLE 2: EDUCATION
YOUR RIGHT: CHILDREN

3.120 You have a right not to be denied access to the educational system, and a right to an effective education. Education embraces the whole process where adults seek to transmit their beliefs, culture and other values to children.

3.121 Teaching means the transmission of knowledge and intellectual development. This right is not necessarily confined to the education of children at school.

YOUR RIGHTS: PARENTS

3.122 Parents have a right to make sure that their religious or philosophical beliefs are respected when public bodies provide education or teaching to their children. This important concept is reflected in the current UK laws on education. For example, Rastafarian parents may claim that their school-age children do not have to cut their hair.

3.123 The fact that a parent's wishes are a minority does not necessarily mean that the majority's view prevails. A balance must be achieved which ensures a fair and proper treatment of minority views. Any abuse of a dominant position is to be avoided.

3.124 But parents cannot stop schools teaching about things like sex education if they are reasonable things for the school to teach, so long as it is not trying to indoctrinate the children. However, parents can remove their children from sex education classes.

LIMITS ON THE RIGHT TO EDUCATION

3.125 The general right to education is not an absolute right to learn whatever you want, whenever you want. The Government has made a special reservation for the European Convention on Human Rights in this area so that education provided by the state is limited to the extent that this is necessary to provide an efficient education and within public spending limits. You might not have a right to the most expensive form of education if there are cheaper alternatives available, but the Government or local education authority must balance the right not to be deprived of an education against the spending limits it imposes. Our Government has stressed that the cost of providing education is a relevant factor in making these decisions.

PUNISHMENTS IN SCHOOLS

3.126 Schools may legitimately impose penalties (providing they do not amount to ill-treatment within Article 3) [Article 3 of the Act states that "no one shall be subjected to torture or to inhuman or degrading treatment or punishment"] on pupils as a form of discipline. A school which imposes a penalty on a pupil will have to show that such a penalty was necessary and a proportionate punishment.

3.127 A purely educational sanction (such as an exclusion) may be acceptable provided it does not breach the parents' rights to ensure the education conforms to their own religious and philosophical convictions.

3.128 Under the Human Rights Act the right to education under Protocol 1, Article 2 may be relevant to areas such as:
• Special educational needs provision
• Access to, or expulsion or exclusion of children from, schools
• (when taken with Article 14) [Article 14 of the Act states that, "the enjoyment of the rights and freedoms set forth in this Convention shall be secured without discrimination on any ground such as sex, race, colour, language, religion, political or other opinion, national or social origin, association with a national minority, property, birth or other status"] the provision of, or exclusion from, education which is discriminatory as between sexes, races or other categories.

In its short September 2000 Guidance Leaflet, *"The Human Rights Act and your school"*, the DfEE states that, *"A well-run school, which follows DfEE guidance on admissions, exclusions and special educational needs, will have nothing to fear".* The DfEE leaflet points out that the Human Rights Act 1998 applies to schools and, therefore, *"Governing bodies, head teachers and local education authorities are, therefore, under a legal obligation to ensure that neither they nor their schools act in a way that contravenes the*

Convention". The DfEE suggests the rights most likely to affect schools are: (1) the right to education; (2) the right to a fair trial; (3) the prohibition of discrimination on the grounds of sex, race, disability or other status; (4) the right to freedom of thought, conscience and religion; (5) the right to privacy and family life; (6) the right to property; and (7) the right to freedom of expression.

The DfEE leaflet suggests ways in which schools (and teachers) should act to avoid risks of legal challenge under the Act. For example:

- the DfEE states that although Article 6 (the right to a fair trial) is not directly applicable to a civil proceeding such as exclusion, existing guidance is that a discipline committee or appeal panel should hear from the pupils themselves if they wish to be heard;
- the DfEE states that random searches of pupils or their belongings should not be carried out as this would contravene Article 8 (the right to privacy);

It should also be remembered that the Human Rights Act 1998 affects teachers as individuals. The three area areas most likely to affect teachers as individuals are: (1) the right to respect for private and family life; (2) the right to freedom of thought, conscience and religion; and (3) the right to a fair trial. If a teacher experiences a problem or a difficulty that they believe falls with the remit of the Human Rights Act 1995, they should contact the legal department of their union for advice.

34. The Protection from Harassment Act 1997

The purpose of the Protection from Harassment Act 1997 is *"to make provision for protecting persons from harassment and similar conduct"*. Although an important aim of the legislation is to help prevent "stalking" (here defined as the obsessive following of another person), the Act's remit goes significantly wider.

The basic premise of the Protection from Harassment Act 1997, which is stated in Section 1, is that, *"A person must not pursue a course of conduct (a) which amounts to harassment of another, and (b) which he knows or ought to know amounts to harassment of the other"*. There are several exceptions (such as that a course of conduct was pursued for the purpose of preventing or detecting crime or in the interests of national security). However, the exceptions are few and, under the Act, *"a person who pursues a course of conduct in breach of section 1 is guilty of an offence"*. Under the Act, harassment is unlawful even if the harasser did not intend harassment; the prosecution only has to prove that a reasonable person would have regarded the behaviour as harassment.

In the Protection of Harassment Act 1997, the definition of "harassing a person" include alarming the person or causing the person distress, and a "course of conduct" (and "conduct" includes speech) must involve conduct on at least two occasions.

Furthermore, putting people in fear of violence is a particularly serious offence under the Act. *"A person whose course of conduct causes another to fear, on at least two occasions, that violence will be used against him is guilty of an offence if he knows or to fear on each of those occasions"* and the penalty on conviction of the offence of causing another to fear violence will be used against him is severe (a fine and/or up to five years in prison).

Although they should be aware of the Protection from Harassment Act 1997, if teachers act professionally then they are unlikely to fall foul of harassment legislation. However, it is wise always to avoid any conduct that could be construed as harassment under the Act. If a teacher is ever accused of such behaviour they should contact the legal department of their union immediately.

Furthermore, if a teacher believes that he/she has been, or is being, harassed (for example, by a colleague or by a parent) in the way that the term is defined in the Protection from Harassment Act 1997, then it would be sensible for the teacher to: (a) discuss it with a senior colleague (if this is appropriate); (b) seek the advice of the legal department of their union; and (c) consider reporting it to the police (because all such behaviour is a criminal offence under the Act).

35. The Public Interest Disclosure Act 1998

This legislation followed the work of Lord Nolan's Committee on Standards in Public Life. The Public Interest Disclosure Act 1998 (sometimes, misleadingly, termed the "Whistleblowing Act") came into force in 1999. The Act is designed: "to protect individuals who make certain disclosures of information in the public interest; to allow such individuals to bring action in respect of victimisation; and for connected purposes". The Act should promote greater openness between workers and employers and, for a worker who discloses malpractice in his/her organisation, it provides protection from detriment and unfair dismissal.

The Public Interest Disclosure Act 1998 stipulates certain criteria which workers have to meet in order to get protection under the Act. The term "worker" has a broader definition than "employee" and, under the Act, the term "worker" applies to: individuals employed under a contract of employment; agency workers; those on work experience linked to a training course or programme; etc. Both teachers and students on courses of initial teacher training, therefore, fall within one of these definitions of worker.

Under the Public Interest Disclosure Act 1998, the information disclosed must be a "qualifying disclosure". What this means is that the worker must have a reasonable belief that the information disclosed tends to show one or more of the following:

- that a criminal offence had been committed, is being committed or is likely to be committed;
- that a person has failed, is failing or is likely to fail to comply with legal obligation to which he is subject;
- that a miscarriage of justice has occurred, is occurring or is likely to occur;

- that the health or safety of any individual has been, is being or is likely to be endangered;
- that the environment has been, is being or is likely to be damaged; or
- that information tending to show any matter falling within any one of the preceding paragraphs has been, is being or is likely to be deliberately concealed.

In cases of exceptionally serious disclosures (for example, the sexual abuse of a child) the Public Interest Disclosure Act 1998 gives a special degree of protection. In this context, a qualifying disclosure is made if: (a) the worker makes the disclosure in good faith, (b) he reasonably believes that the information disclosed, and any allegation contained in it, are substantially true, (c) he does not make disclosure for the purposes of personal gain. (d) the relevant failure is of an exceptionally serious nature, an (e) in all circumstances of the case, it is reasonable for him to make the disclosure.

Workers who make a disclosure in accordance with the Public Interest Disclosure Act 1998's conditions have the legal right not to be subject to any detriment. The Act protects such workers from both dismissal and victimisation; this also includes a failure to promote or withholding a salary rise.

It is, however, extremely important to note that – to maintain his/her protection under the Act - a worker who sees or suspects misconduct or fraud, a public danger, or some other serious malpractice is, in most cases, only permitted to make the disclosure to their employer, to a legal advisor, or to any other party to whom the relevant failure relates. A teacher in such a situation should very quickly seek advice from the legal department of their union.

36. The Copyright, Designs and Patents Act 1988

The Copyright, Designs and Patents Act 1988 was put on the list of documents in the DfES/TTA's 2002 *"Guidance on the Standards for Qualified Teacher Status"* at the specific request of the Publishers Association. The Publishers Association (and the Department of Trade and Industry) are anxious to stress, the importance of observation of the laws of copyright throughout the educational system.

Copyright provides legal protection to authors, playwrights, composers, etc. so that they can control and benefit from the way in which their intellectual property is used and exploited. Copyright protection lasts for decades, for example: literary, dramatic, musical, artistic works (including computer programs, tables and compilations), films and video recordings, normally last up to seventy years from the end of the year of death of the author/creator.

Although modern technological devices (such as photocopiers, tape recording machines, video recorder machines, computers, etc.) make the copying of materials extremely easy, it is highly likely that the original material (document, music, film, etc.) is, in fact, protected by copyright and it is usually unlawful to infringe copyright. Thus, if material is protected by copyright (be it a book, play, musical score, music recording, video recording, computer disk, computer programme, etc.), it is usually unlawful to make a copy of the material without making a payment or obtaining the express permission of the author, playwright, composer, etc.

However, the Copyright, Designs and Patents Act 1988 does allow reasonable access to copy material for educational purposes. The relevant sections of the Act are: Sections 32 to 36 inc. (Education) and Section 116 (Licensing schemes and licensing bodies). Section 32 is a general statement concerning copying for purposes of instruction or examination - and it is worth noting that any such copying does not include copying by means of a reprographic process; Section 33 deals with the copying of anthologies for educational use; Section 34 deals with the performing, playing or showing work in the course of activities of an educational establishment; Section 35 deals with recording of broadcasts and cable programmes by educational establishments; Section 36 deals with the reprographic copying of passages from published works - and it is worth noting that not more than one per cent (1%) of any work may be copied in any three month period; and Section 116 deals with licensing schemes and licensing bodies. It is important to note also that the educational use is strictly defined. If material is "dealt with" (i.e. sold, let for hire, or offered or exposed for sale or hire) then the copying is deemed to be an infringement of the copyright.

However, teachers should note that – through the Copyright Licensing Agency – there is a scheme for the licensed copying of books, periodicals and journals for educational purposes. Each maintained school should have a copy of both the agreement and its operational instructions. It is important that teachers and schools adhere closely to the provisions of the scheme. (At the time of writing, this scheme did not apply to schools in the non-maintained independent sector.)

37. Mental Health in Education: Promoting Children's Mental Health within Early Years and School Settings, DfES 2001

The June 2001 DfES Guidance document "*Promoting Children's Mental Health within Early Years and School Settings*" is a very substantial 64-page publication. However, there is also a December 2001 4-page summary DfES Guidance document (with the same title). Both may be obtained from the DfES Publications Department (tel. 0846-602-2260) (free of charge) or via the DfES website (www.dfes.gov.uk).

In June 2001 the government issued its good practice guidance on "*Promoting Children's Mental Health within Early Years and School Settings*" as part of a wider government strategy to raise educational standards for all children, to tackle the causes of social exclusion, and to transform children's services. Schools, often working in partnership with other agencies, can help promote the mental health of all children, and particularly those children most at risk of developing mental health problems. The DfES publications offer pointers and examples of good practice to help school staff, working alongside mental health professionals, in early identification and intervention for pupils experiencing mental health problems. (All passages quoted verbatim below are from the December 2001 4-page Summary document.)

It needs to be pointed out that increasing numbers of children are experiencing mental health problems. (One survey, quoted in the DfES document, showed that ten per cent of children between five and fifteen experience clinically defined mental health problems.) Therefore, sooner or later, teachers are going to meet - and will have to deal with - children with mental health problems.

The mental health problems in children and young people, as defined by mental health professionals, are:

- emotional disorders e.g. phobias, anxiety states and depression;

- conduct disorders e.g. stealing, defiance, fire-setting, aggression and anti-social behaviour;
- hyperkinetic disorders e.g. disturbance of activity and attention;
- developmental disorders e.g. delay in acquiring certain skills as speech, social ability or bladder control, primarily affecting children with autism and those with pervasive developmental disorders;
- attachment disorders e.g. children who are markedly distressed or socially impaired as a result of an extremely abnormal pattern of attachment to parents or major carers;
- other mental health problems including eating disorders, habit disorders, post-traumatic stress syndromes; somatic disorders; and psychotic disorders e.g. schizophrenia and manic depressive disorder.

Some of these problems may be mild and transitory whilst others are serious and long lasting. Schools need to understand a child's needs to decide what help and support might be most useful. The sorts of questions to be asked might include:

- What sort of problem is the child presenting?
- What is the impact of the child's problem?
- Risks. What factors have initiated and maintained the problem?
- Strengths. What assets are there to work with?
- Are there wider perspectives?

It should be pointed out that the *"Special Educational Needs Code of Practice"*, DfES 2002 (in the Special Educational Needs/Disability section in this booklet, see the chapter on the Special Educational Needs Code of Practice), contains clear guidance for meeting children's needs, including those children who have emotional and behavioural difficulties and mental health problems.

The DfES points out that promoting children's mental health within schools has important educational payoffs, resulting in improved academic attainments for all children. The DfES states:

Early Years Settings
Characteristics of Early Years Settings that actively promote the emotional well-being of children. These include:

- stable child care relationships so that children interact with just a few primary care givers in any one day;
- low staff turnover so that children are cared for by the same individuals over several years;
- good staff training in staff development;
- adequate staff to child ratios; and
- positive behaviour management.

Schools

Key characteristics of schools that promote their children and young people's mental health share:

- a committed senior management team, creating a culture within the school in which the importance of trust, integrity, democracy, equality of opportunity and each child being valued regardless of their ability is seen as being vital;
- a culture within the school which values teachers, lunchtime supervisors, and all those engaged in the care and supervision of children;
- clear policies on vital issues such as behaviour and bullying – 'whole school behaviour' policies which set out the range of acceptable behaviour for children, and what is not acceptable;
- the range of sanctions that will result and the acceptance and implementation of the policies throughout the school;
- high professional standards (efficient planning, setting, marking, punctuality);
- skilful teaching which arouses pupil interest and motivates; and
- proactive work with parents.

The DfES suggests practices and strategies in pre-school settings and primary and secondary schools that all teachers can use to support children with mental health problems. These are:

- In the classroom – Through clear effective whole class management and work with small groups of children or individual children to promote their behaviour, social development and self-esteem;
- In the playground – Through schemes to help children at these potentially difficult times;

- Out of school through effective links with parents – Some schools offer schemes to support parents to better manage their children's behaviour, alongside work being carried out with the child at school. Such support can be very effective in helping vulnerable children.

It must be stressed that the December 2001 4-page summary document clearly cannot provide anything like the same detail as the June 2001 64-page substantive document. Therefore, it is important that reference is made to the June 2001 DfES document *"Promoting Children's Mental Health within Early Years and School Settings"*. To provide a flavour of what the substantive DfES document contains, the headings of the five sections and what they contain are reproduced below. (There is also a Foreword, Introduction, Appendix containing Case Studies, and Bibliography.)

Section 1 Questions about Mental Health: (1) What is Mental Health? (2) Mental Health or Emotional and Behavioural Difficulty? (3) What are the Causes of mental Health Problems in Children and Young People?

Section 2 Whole School Approaches to Promoting Children's Mental Health: (1) Good Practice in Schools (2) Early Years Settings (3) Primary and Secondary School Settings.

Section 3 Interventions to Support Individual who are Experiencing Difficulties: (1) Understanding Individual Children's Needs (2) Early Intervention in Early Years Settings (3) Early Interventions in Primary Schools (4) Early Interventions in Secondary Schools.

Section 4 Specific Mental Health Problems and Useful Approaches that Schools can take: (1) Conduct Disorders/Problems (2) Attention Deficit/Hyperactivity (3) Emotional Disorders (4) Compulsive Obsessive Disorders (5) Anorexia Nervosa & Bulimia Nervosa (6) Deliberate Self-Harm/Suicidal Behaviour (7) Asperger's Syndrome/Autistic Spectrum Disorders.

Section 5 Support for Schools: (1) Education Staff Working in Schools (2) Other Professionals Working in Schools (3) Specialist Educational Support (4) Health Professionals Working in Schools (5) Social Services Staff with a Remit to Support Children at Risk (6) Health Staff Operating outside School (7) Specialist Mental Health Professionals.

Other information, guidance and legislation which teachers should be aware of

38. The Induction Period for Newly Qualified Teachers

Section 19 of the Teaching and Higher Education Act 1998, and the Education (Induction Arrangements for School Teachers) (England) Regulations 1999, introduced the statutory arrangements that provide all newly qualified teachers (NQTs) with a bridge from initial teacher training to effective professional practice. These statutory arrangements do not change the fact that Qualified Teacher Status (QTS) is awarded at the successful completion of initial teacher training. However, **Newly Qualified Teachers who are awarded Qualified Teacher Status and who do not complete satisfactorily the statutory induction period will, thereafter, not be eligible for employment as a teacher in a maintained school or in a non-maintained special school, in England.**

Since 7th May 1999, all teachers who obtain Qualified Teacher Status, including those who follow employment-based programmes, must complete successfully the statutory induction period of three terms (or equivalent) if they are to work as teachers in maintained primary or secondary schools, or in non-maintained special schools in England. (If a newly qualified teacher fails the statutory induction period and, thereafter, cannot work as a teacher in a maintained primary or secondary school, or in a non-maintained special school, he/she still retains Qualified Teacher Status because Qualified Teacher Status is awarded once a course of initial teacher training has been completed successfully.)

There is no time limit for starting the induction period although it is expected that newly qualified teachers will normally complete their induction period within five years of starting it. For newly qualified teachers who wish initially to work as supply teachers, the supply period in a school can count but only if a teacher is working for periods of one term or more and the head teacher agrees at the outset. In the case of part-time work, the length of the induction period depends on the proportion of the week that is being worked; for example, if a newly qualified teacher works 50% of each week then the length of the induction period will need to last for six terms.

DfES Guidance document 582/2001, which is only available on the Internet at the DfES website (www.dfes.gov.uk) describes in detail the induction standards against which newly qualified teachers will be assessed, the schools which can provide a period of induction, and gives guidance on how head teachers and other school staff should support, monitor and assess newly qualified teachers during their first year of teaching. (During their induction period, newly qualified teachers have a reduced timetable of 90% of the teaching duties of teachers in their school who do not have points of responsibility.) The DfES Guidance document also covers unsatisfactory progress, extensions (only granted in exceptional circumstances) and the appeal arrangements if a teacher fails the final assessment.

It is important to note that although the vast majority of newly qualified teachers will complete their induction period successfully, a newly qualified teacher only has one chance of induction. This is an important document and newly qualified teachers would all be advised to read it. (The Teacher Training Agency also provides guidance materials on the statutory induction period for newly qualified teachers and those completing their courses of initial teacher training.)

It is worthwhile reproducing Annex A of DfES Guidance document 582/2001:

Standards for determining whether an NQT has satisfactorily completed an Induction Period.

1.   In order to recommend that a NQT has satisfactorily completed the induction period, the head teacher should be satisfied that the NQT has:
     a. continued to meet the Standards for the Award of QTS consistently in teaching at the school;
     b. met all the Induction Standards

The Induction Standards

2.   To meet the Induction Standards, the NQT should demonstrate that he or she:

Planning, Teaching and Class Management

a. sets clear targets for improvement of pupils' achievement, monitors pupils' progress towards those targets and uses appropriate teaching strategies in the light of this, including, where appropriate, in relation to literacy, numeracy and other school targets;

b. plans effectively to ensure that pupils have the opportunity to meet their potential, notwithstanding differences of race and gender, and taking into account of the needs of pupils who are:

- underachieving;
- very able
- not yet fluent in English.

Making use of relevant information and specialist help where available.

c. secures a good standard of pupil behaviour in the classroom through establishing appropriate rules and high expectations of discipline which pupils respect, acting to pre-empt and deal with inappropriate behaviour in the context of the behaviour policy of the school;

d. plans effectively, where applicable, to meet the needs of pupils with Special Educational Needs and, in collaboration with the SENCO, makes an appropriate contribution to the preparation, monitoring and review of Individual Education Plans;

e. takes account of ethnic and cultural diversity to enrich the curriculum and raise achievement.

Monitoring, Assessment, Recording, Reporting and Accountability

f. recognises the level that a pupil is achieving and makes accurate assessments, independently, against attainment targets, where applicable, and performance levels associated with other tests or qualifications relevant to the subject(s) or phase(s) taught;

g. liases effectively with pupils' parents/carers through informative oral and written reports on pupils' progress and achievements, discussing appropriate targets, and encouraging them to support their children's learning, behaviour and progress.

Other Professional Requirements

h. where applicable, deploys support staff and other adults effectively in the classroom, involving them, where appropriate, in the planning and management of pupils' learning;

i. takes responsibility for implementing school policies and practices, including those dealing with bullying and racial harassment;

j. takes responsibility for their own professional development, setting objectives for improvements, and taking action to keep up-to-date with research and developments in pedagogy and in the subject(s) they teach.

The Induction Standards also state that, to complete induction successfully, the NQT must have passed the three Qualified Teacher Status Skills Tests for teacher training candidates (i.e. numeracy, literacy, and information and communications technology).

39. The General Teaching Council for England

For many years teachers and those concerned with education have been pressing governments to allow the teaching profession to have its own independent body – a Council of teachers and other experienced persons concerned with education – to help shape the profession in the best interests of children and teachers. The Teaching and Higher Education Act 1998 finally contained the legislation for the establishment of General Teaching Councils for England and Wales and (later) Northern Ireland; (Scotland has had a General Teaching Council since 1966). The establishment of the General Teaching Council for England took place on 1st September 2000. The aims of the General Teaching Council for England (set out in 2000) are to: (a) raise the professional status and public standing of teachers; (b) provide an independent and influential voice for teachers; and (c) maintain and guarantee high professional standards of teaching.

It is important that all teachers know what the General Teaching Council for England is, because **to teach in a maintained school or non-maintained special school, it is a statutory requirement to be registered with the General Teaching Council.** Furthermore, the General Teaching Council for England has substantial power and (just like the doctors' General Medical Council) the General Teaching Council for England has the power to **remove a teacher from the register** if it finds them guilty of either serious professional misconduct or incompetence.

Furthermore, newly qualified teachers should know that it is to the General Teaching Council for England that the "Appropriate Body" (normally the local education authority) makes its report on whether or not the newly qualified teacher has met the Induction Standards at the end of the statutory induction period. If the Appropriate Body informs the General Teaching Council for England that the newly qualified teacher has failed to meet the induction standards, then the General Teaching Council for England will remove the teacher's name from the Register of Teachers. Furthermore, if the newly qualified teacher wishes to appeal against this decision, the General Teaching Council for England is the "Appeal Body". When the appeal has taken place, the decision of the General Teaching Council for England (as the Appeal Body) is final.

In this booklet, in the section Other Relevant Documents, the chapter on the General Teaching Council and the *"Code of Professional Values and Practice for Teachers"* describes the General Teaching Council Code which teachers must observe. Further information on the General Teaching Council for England may be obtained from the GTC (tel. 0870–001–0308) or from the GTC website (www.gtce.org.uk).

40. The Employment Relations Act 1999

The Employment Relations Act 1999 is a very significant piece of employment legislation and it contains a broad package of measures that benefits millions of employees, including part-time workers, mothers-to-be and adoptive parents. The Act makes significant changes to three particular areas of employment law: (a) unfair dismissal and individual rights; (b) family friendly rights (including maternity leave and parental leave); and (c) collective rights (including trade union recognition and the right to be represented at disciplinary and grievance hearings).

Because a large and growing proportion of the teaching profession are female, the Act's maternity legislation is extremely important and, furthermore, the legislation for part-time workers is also well worth noting as more and more teachers opt to work on a part-time basis.

The six main features of the family friendly rights section of the Act are:

(1)   "Ordinary Maternity Leave" (which used to be termed Maternity Leave), to which all women are entitled, is increased from 14 weeks to 18 weeks so as to match the period of time during which women are entitled to Statutory Maternity Pay;

(2)   "Compulsory Maternity Leave" of 2 weeks, the two weeks which follow the baby's birth, (and any employer who allows a woman to work during this two week period will be guilty of a criminal offence);

(3)   "Additional Maternity Leave" which covers the period from the end of the 18 weeks Ordinary Maternity Leave period to 29 weeks after the baby's birth. As now, women entitled to Additional Maternity Leave will be allowed to take a total of

40 weeks maternity leave but the right to Additional Maternity Leave will apply after only 1 year's service (rather than 2
years' service);

(4)   "Parental Leave" entitlement which permits parents to take 3
months' unpaid leave in order to care for a child (although
some qualifications apply) and this also applies to adopted
children;

(5)   "Leave for Family and Domestic Reasons" entitlement which
gives employees the right to take a reasonable amount of
unpaid time off work to deal with a domestic incident(s); and

(6)   by implementing the EU Directive on part-time work, the Act
also tackles discrimination against part-time workers. Any
instance of discrimination against part-time workers will
need to be justified by the employer.

41. The Working Time Regualtions 1998

The European Working Time Directive 1991, implemented in United Kingdom domestic law in the Working Time Regulations 1998, is very unlikely to affect teachers because the Conditions of Employment of Teachers (other than head teachers) already ensures that the teacher's working hours and work patterns are well within the Working Time Regulations 1998 guidelines.

However, heads, deputy heads and assistant heads frequently have to work much longer hours than other teachers. In such cases the law makes clear that where an employee (e.g. a head or deputy head) decides what the working time will be, or has autonomous decision making powers, then that staff group can be exempted by means of derogations by Regulations or by collective agreements. So even very busy heads and deputy heads are most unlikely to be affected by the Working Time Regulations 1998.

The aim of the Working Time Regulations 1998 is to ensure that workers are protected against adverse effects on their health and safety caused by working excessively long hours, having inadequate rest or disrupted work patterns.

The Working Time Regulations 1998 provides for:

(a)   a maximum 48 hours working week, averaged over a 17 week reference period;

(b)   a minimum daily rest period of 11 consecutive hours a day;

(c)   a rest break of at least 20 minutes where the working day is longer than 6 hours;

(d)   a minimum rest day of one day a week;

(e)   a statutory right to paid annual holiday; and

(f)   night working (between 2300 and 0600) cannot exceed an average of 8 hours in any 24 hour period.

As can be seen, most teachers are very unlikely to be affected. However, schools may need to consider the position of school caretakers or security guards (where a permanent presence is needed).

42. The Part-Time Workers (Prevention of Less Favourable Treatment) Regulations 2000, and the Fixed-Term Employees (Prevention of Less Favourable Treatment) Regulations 2002

As many teachers work on a part-time or fixed-term basis, it is worth looking briefly at these two pieces of legislation. The Part-Time Workers (Prevention of Less Favourable Treatment) Regulations 2000 prohibits discrimination against part-time workers unless the treatment is justified on objective grounds.

Basically, a part-time worker must not be treated less favourably than a comparable full-time worker either in the terms of his/her contract or in terms of being subjected to any other detriment. Part-time workers are now entitled to receive the same: (a) rate of pay; (b) promotion and training opportunities; (c) sick pay and maternity rights; (d) access to occupational pension schemes; (e) entitlements to annual holiday, etc; and (f) parental leave and career break schemes. If a part-time worker believes that he/she may have been discriminated against on the basis that he/she works part-time, then he/she has to find a comparable full-time worker with which to compare the terms and conditions of his/her employment. The worker must be: (a) employed by the same employer as the comparator; (b) be under the same type of contract; and (c) on broadly similar work.

The Fixed-Term Employees (Prevention of Less Favourable Treatment) Regulations 2002 is aimed at preventing discrimination against temporary/fixed-term staff and to prevent abuse arising from the use of successive fixed-term contracts. The new Regulations allow workers on fixed-term contracts to claim equality of treatment with their permanent colleagues (such as pay and benefits). There are several new rights for fixed-term employees including: (a) an entitlement to be informed by the employer of available vacancies in the establishment; (b) the prohibition of 'redundancy waiver clauses' (for any contracts made or renewed after 10th July 2002); and (c) a right to conversion to permanent status once the employee has served on successive fixed-term contracts continuously for four years (the four years starting from July 2002). Furthermore, in a possible redundancy situation (and providing they have been employed for at least one year), the fixed-term worker has the same employment rights as their permanent colleagues. However, these Fixed-Term Employees (Prevention of Less Favourable Treatment) Regulations 2002 do not provide any protection for staff employed through an agency. Teachers employed through the teaching agencies continue to have no security of employment or any pension rights. (It is worth noting that the European Union is discussing a possible Directive for Temporary Agency Workers to give agency workers equal rights after a qualifying period of work in one establishment. No doubt it will take considerable time before any legislation results).

43. The Data Protection Act 1998

The Data Protection Act 1998 came into force in March 2000. The Act requires that "data controllers" (those that hold data on others) should be registered and the way in which this data is obtained, held, and used should comply with the eight principles of the Act. Anyone on whom data is held is a "data subject" and "data processing" refers to any action involving data, including simply holding that data in a form from which it can be retrieved.

The eight principles embodying the fundamental purpose of the Data Protection Act 1998 require that data must be:

- fairly and lawfully processed
- processed for limited purposes (particularly sensitive data)
- adequate, relevant and not excessive;
- accurate
- not kept for longer than necessary
- processed in accordance with the rights of the data subject
- kept with adequate security, and
- not transferred to countries outside the European Economic Area unless the territory ensures an adequate level of protection.

Whereas the previous Data Protection Act 1984 was concerned with personal data held in a computer system, the Data Protection Act 1998 applies to manual records held in a "relevant filing system" as well as to computer records

Clearly schools, both as employers and as educational establishments, contain large amounts of data (on staff and pupils etc.). Teachers should be aware of the Data Protection Act 1998 and always ensure that they comply with its requirements. Information on the Act can be obtained from the Data Protection website (www.dataprotection.gov.uk).

44. Reference Writing - a word of caution

On occasions, teachers have to write references; these may be for col-leagues or friends or regarding pupils (e.g. UCAS forms). It is well worth noting the 1994 landmark case of *Spring -v- Guardian Assurance* which those who write references should always bear in mind. In this case, the House of Lords ruled that an employer who gave a reference in respect of a former employee owed that employee a duty to take reasonable care in its preparation and would be liable to him in negligence if he failed to do so and the employee suffered economic loss. As far as teachers are con-cerned, the principle of vicarious liability would be likely to apply, unless the teacher is writing the reference outside the employment situation (such as writing a reference for a friend).

Those who write references, be they for employees, colleagues or pupils, must take due care in the preparation of the references to ensure that they are accurate. If it can be shown that, as a result of the negligent (careless) preparation of a reference, a person of whom it was written suf-fers any financial loss (eg not being offered the post for which they applied) then the aggrieved person could probably successfully claim damages.

Anything written in a reference must be true and should, if necessary, be able to be substantiated. This applies as much to a reference that is a "glowing tribute" as well as to a reference that may be less than favourable. If in doubt, think carefully whether you should, in fact, write the refer-ence. However, failure to decline to write a reference could, in itself, be damaging. Always be prudent and, if in any doubt, do not hesitate to ask for advice from a senior colleague or your union.

A reference writer should make it quite clear to the subject of the ref-erence (some schools and colleges already do this) that they will only pro-vide one if the subject accepts that there will be a disclaimer of liability to the subject and to the recipient. Such a disclaimer might read: *"Confidential: For your private use and without responsibility on the part of xyz".*

Bibliography

ATL *Taking Students Off-Site*, 2000

CRE *Code of Practice for the Elimination of Racial Discrimination in Employment*, 1984

DfE & DH *The Education of Children with Emotional and Behavioural Difficulties*, DfE Circular 9/94 & DHLAC (94) 9, May 1994

DfEE *Protecting Children from Abuse: the Role of the Education Service*, Circular 10/95, October 1995

DfEE *Misconduct of Teachers and Workers with Children and Young Persons*, Circular 11/95, October 1995 (NB document discontinued)

DfEE *Supporting Pupils with Medical Needs*, DfEE Good Practice Guide, 1996

DfEE *What the Disability Discrimination Act (DDA) 1995 means for Schools and LEAs*, DfEE Circular 3/97, March 1997 (NB document discontinued)

DfEE *Section 550A of The Education Act 1996: The Use of Force to Control or Restrain Pupils*, DfEE Circular 10/98, July 1998

DfEE *Recruitment and Selection Procedures: Vetting Teachers and Other Staff who will have Contact with Children*, DfEE Guidance Note 10/9/98, September 1998 (NB document discontinued)

DfEE *Physical and Mental Fitness to Teach of Teachers and of Entrants to Initial Teacher Training*, DfEE Circular 4/99, May 1999

DfEE *Social Inclusion: Pupil Support*, DfEE Circular 10/99, July 1999

DfEE *The Human Rights Act and your school*, DfEE Guidance leaflet, September 2000, DfEE 0194/2000

DfEE *Preventing Unsuitable People from Working with Children and Young Persons*, DfEE, October 2000

DfEE *Education of Young People in Public Care*, DfEE Guidance, 2001

DfEE & DH *Supporting Pupils with Medical Needs in School*, DfEE Circular

14/96, October 1996

DfES *Health and Safety of Pupils on Educational Visits*, DfES Good Practice Guide, DfES 1998.

DfES *The Induction Period for Newly Qualified Teachers*, DfES Guidance July 2001, DfES 582/2001

DfES *Promoting Children's Mental Health within Early Years and School Settings*, DfES June 2001, DfEE 0121/2001

DfES *Promoting Children's Mental Health within Early Years and School Settings*, DfES Guidance, December 2001, DfES 0619/2002

DfES *Special Educational Needs Code of Practice*, DfES, November 2000

DfES & TTA *Handbook to the Guidance on Standards for the Award of Qualified Teacher Status*, DfEE & TTA, 2002

DfES & TTA *Qualifying to Teach: Professional Standards for Qualified Teacher Status and Requirements for Initial Teacher Training*, TPU 0803/02-02

DH, HO & DfEE *Working Together to Safeguard Children: A guide to inter-agency working to safeguard and promote the welfare of children*, 1999

GTC *Code of Professional Values and Practice for Teachers*, 2002

HMSO *Equal Pay Act 1970*

HMSO *Health and Safety at Work Act 1974*

HMSO *Sex Discrimination Act 1975*

HMSO *Race Relations Act 1976*

HMSO *Copyright, Designs and Patents Act 1988*

HMSO *Children Act 1989*

HMSO *School Teachers' Pay and Conditions Act 1991*

HMSO *Disability Discrimination Act 1995*

HMSO *Education Act 1996*

HMSO *Education Act 1997*

HMSO *Protection from Harassment Act 1997*

HMSO *Data Protection Act 1998*

HMSO *Human Rights Act 1998*

HMSO *Public Interest Disclosure Act 1998*

HMSO *Working Time Regulations 1998*

HMSO *Employment Relations Act 1999*

HMSO *Race Relations Act 1976*

HMSO *Race Relations (Amendment) Act 2000*

HMSO *Part-Time Workers (Prevention of Less Favourable Treatment) Regulations 2000*

HMSO *Sexual Offences (Amendment) Act 2000*

HMSO *Special Educational Needs and Disability Act 2001*

HMSO *Fixed-Term Employees (Prevention of Less Favourable Treatment) Regulations 2002*

HMSO *School Teachers' Pay and Conditions Document 2002*

HO *Caring for young people and the vulnerable? Guidance for preventing abuse of trust*, 1999

HO *Study Guide: Human Rights Act 1998*, October 2000

Lowe, C. *Teachers' Rights, Duties and Responsibilities*, 5th Edition 2001, Croner CCH

OFSTED *Raising the Attainment of Minority Ethnic Pupils – School and LEA Responses*, 1999

OFSTED *Evaluating Educational Inclusion – Guidance for Inspectors and Schools*, 2000

TTA *Raising the Attainment of Minority Ethnic Pupils*, 2000

TTA *Guidance on the Requirements for Initial Teacher Training*, April 2002

TTA *Handbook on the Introduction to the Guidance on the Standards for the Award of Qualified Teacher Status*, June 2002

TTA *Into Induction 2002: An introduction for Trainee Teachers to the Induction Period for Newly Qualified Teachers*, TTA 2002, TPU 0805/2-02

TUC *Your Rights at Work*, Kogan Page, 2000

ATL = Association of Teachers and Lecturers
CRE = Council for Racial Equality
DfE = Department for Education
DfEE = Department for Education and Employment
DfES = Department for Education and Skills
DH = Department of Health
GTC = General Teaching Council for England
HO = Home Office
HMSO = Her Majesty's Stationery Office
OFSTED = Office for Standards in Education
TTA = Teacher Training Agency
TUC = Trades Union Congress

Index